THE MAN IN YOUR LIFE

In appreciation for your support of Focus on the Family, please accept this copy of *Understanding the Man in Your Life* by H. Norman Wright. Your contributions enable this organization to address the needs of homes through radio, television, literature and counseling.

On the following pages you will find practical advice on how to live in harmony with the man in your life and how to understand the behavior that is uniquely masculine. We trust that this book will make a fine addition to your home library.

Focus on the Family
Pomona, CA 91799

Understanding the Man in Your Life

H. Norman Wright

WORD BOOKS
PUBLISHER
WACO, TEXAS

A DIVISION OF
WORD, INCORPORATED

Library of Congress Cataloging in Publication Data

Wright, H. Norman.
    Understanding the man in your life.

    Includes bibliographies.
    1. Men—Psychology. 2. Sex role. 3. Masculinity
(Psychology) I. Title.
HQ1090.W75   1987   305.3'1   87–2177
ISBN 0–8499–0609–1

89801239 FG 98765432

Printed in the United States of America

This book is dedicated to the three women of my life
who have encouraged me, believed in me,
supported me and shared with me their love.

> My mother, *Amelia Wright,*
> my wife, *Joycelin,*
> and my daughter, *Sheryl.*

To each of them I would like to express
my thankfulness for their lives
and pray God's continued blessing upon them.

Contents

Understanding the Man in Your Life

1

What Is a Man?

"I am a man. I am now a middle-aged man. In many ways, I am not sure that I am typical of other men, and in other ways I am typical (I hope). I am different than I was twenty years ago and I will be different twenty years from now. In the dictionary, Webster defines me as: 'A human being; an adult male human; a bipedal primate mammal, that is anatomically related to the great apes; the quality or state of being manly.' I hope I am more than that."

What is it really like to be a man? Are men tough and unemotional machines who relate best to the dog-eat-dog world of business? Or are they simply little boys who have never really grown up, playing with their grown-up toys and leaving a trail of dirty socks behind them? Are men sensitive to the feelings of others?

Perhaps the best way to find out who men are—and who they are not—is to look at some of the stereotypes about men. To discover these stereotypes, I decided to interview some women to discover their attitudes and beliefs about the male creature. I formulated some questions and with pen in hand I set forth. The results of my survey are both amusing and enlightening.

Question #1: "Is it true that men are little boys who never grow up?" Why would anyone think such a thing?

"I'll tell you why," a wife said to me with intensity and a slight glare. "Men never outgrow their need for toys. They like anything that goes 'ping,' 'beep,' and has rows of lights with switches and anything that says 'batteries not included.' He buys gadgets and adjusts them more in one month than

11

they need in a lifetime. I'd like half as much attention." And with that she walked away. I was kind of sorry I'd asked the question.

Question #2: "Is it true that all men are sports nuts?" Not profiting from my mistake in asking the first question, I ventured this query to another wife.

She looked at me as though some of the bricks were missing in my chimney, hesitated and then said, "Well, I don't know if *all* men are that way . . . but Jim tends to breathe heavier when he talks about sports. In fact, there are times when I could swear that he actually paws the pavement. I think he dreams of the day when a forward pass comes sailing out of the television and he leaps up and intercepts it. I've seen him actually cry when his team lost. And it was a pre-season exhibition game at that! Now, does that answer your question?" I gulped and nodded. So much for my interviews.

Question #3: "Do men tend to be sloppy around the house?" I've heard this idea kicked around quite a bit so I decided to find out for myself. Here are the responses of several women:

"Are you kidding? My husband habitually leaves a half-filled juice glass in the living room and one day I decided I was tired of picking it up. So I left it for three days. In three days I had three half-filled juice glasses with half of a leftover in the most recent one, dead ants in the second, and dead ants, a bloated spider and a dead fly in the first glass.

"My husband doesn't have a den. He has a habitation location which is organized, so he tells me. Whatever organized it probably had a prefrontal lobotomy two decades ago and decided to play room scramble! I don't even like to go into that room. There's probably something living in there and I don't know what it might do to me."

While she was telling me this, her husband was standing there smiling and saying, "She's right, it is that way. But it sure keeps people out of there!" The elbow he nudged her with at that moment was intact, but I began to fear she might render it unusable, judging from the glare she was giving him.

But then I was totally unprepared for some new responses

from several wives. One actually said, "Sloppy! Don't I wish! I'm married to Mr. Clean. I think he has a case of terminal tidies! His clothes are hung in the closet, color coded and a half inch apart. Everything is labeled. If the cat wasn't so fast, it would have a label on it. You'd think we didn't know what anything is without his labels. We bring snacks into the family room and he hovers over us like a hawk because he's so afraid of crumbs. You won't believe this guy. He Windexes the TV screen every day after we watch it! But I've figured it out. I know why he's that way. His mother toilet-trained him too well. I believe that when he was a child his goal in life was to grow up to be the Ty-D-Bol man and tear around the toilet in his sailor suit dispensing chemicals! You laugh!" She continued, "What other man wants his underwear ironed! He wakes me in the middle of the night to ask me if I cleaned the shower and when I mumble 'yes' he asks me if I dried it out and sprayed Lysol. Norm, why are you laughing? It's not funny! It's a serious disease!"

I don't usually laugh like that when I ask questions, but I wasn't prepared for her answer. I tried to find out where she and her husband lived so I could see this place. But to no avail. I wasn't too disappointed since I probably would have had to take off my shoes before I could enter the house—and I knew I had a hole in one sock. I didn't want to be responsible for the trauma that would create for her husband!

A Different Approach

I decided to take a different tack. I would use an open-ended question to sample the concerns of women about men's behavior. So I began to ask wives, "Is there any characteristic or habit your husband has that you would like to change?" Wrong question! I was looking for brief responses, but I got more than I bargained for with that one. Two of the most interesting responses were these:

"Why can't a man put the toilet seat down before he leaves the bathroom? I've mentioned it a hundred times and nothing happens. It's always up even in the middle of the night and when you're half asleep, you can imagine the problems that creates! And why must the bathroom become his personal library? My husband actually asked for a magazine rack for the bathroom as his birthday present last year! If we didn't have two bathrooms, we'd have to take a number around our house."

"Yes! There is something I'd like to change and I think most wives feel this way. Why do men want to fix everything, except what you want them to fix? Even when I'm upset and just want to talk about my feelings, he wants to fix them! I mean, even when he's cooking and accidentally breaks an egg, he looks at it like there ought to be some way to put this thing back together again! If our tropical fish has a defective fin, he's plotting some way to get in there and fix it! The other night I was sitting there watching television and John walked into the room and said, 'It's terrible. It's not right.'

"I said, 'What?'

"'The picture. It's off.'

"'John,' I said, 'it's not off. I've been watching it for an hour and it's fine. Sit down and enjoy the show.'

"'No, that man is too yellow.'

"'No, he isn't and besides he's got a suntan.' But John sat in front of the TV for the next fifteen minutes fiddling with every knob until he had it right. Which was exactly the way I had it! He wants to fix things that are unbroken. He has this incessant drive to repair. I wish someone would fix his desire to fix everything."

After several hours of interviewing women, I didn't know if I had enough valid findings to draw any conclusions or not. But it was interesting. I decided to look elsewhere for some more pertinent data to help discover what we men are really like! I was afraid that even the few women I talked with might be right!

Men Can Be Understood

What do you know about the men in your life? What do you understand about them? The phrase, "I just don't understand that man," is one of the most frequent statements of all! You can understand us. We are not that complex or unusual or weird—we're just different. Our bodies are different and our minds are different. We think and experience life differently than do women. Some differences happen genetically and some are culturally determined. How are men different than women?

Just for openers . . .

Men snore more;
They fight more;
They change their minds more often than women do;
Their blood is redder;
Their daylight vision is superior;
They have thicker skins and longer vocal cords;
Their metabolic rate is higher;
More of them are left-handed;
They feel pain less than women;
They age earlier (unfortunately);
They wrinkle later;
Rich men are fatter than rich women;
Men's immunity against disease is weaker;
Men talk about themselves less;
They worry about themselves more;
They are not as sensitive to others as women are.[1]

Men are constructed differently inside and out! Have you ever heard women complain about men and weight loss? "It isn't fair! Why can my husband lose weight easier than I can? I work and work at it and it's a struggle but it seems to be easier for him and other men." It's sad but true! Men have an easier time losing weight than women do. Why? Because men's fat is distributed differently than women's. Men lack the layer of fat just underneath their skin that women have. They also have more muscle than women, 41 percent to 35 percent. The greater proportion of muscle to fat makes it easier to burn off the fat. One of the sad facts of life!

Some men like to be thought of as a male machine. These men are a special breed different from women, children and other men who don't measure up. The male machine is functional and designed mainly for work. He is programmed in a special way: to tackle jobs, attack problems, override obstacles, overcome challenges and above all, always take the offensive. If any task is presented to him in a competitive manner, he will take it on. And winning and achieving is all the reinforcement

What Is a Man? □ 15

he needs. The armor plating he protects himself with is difficult to penetrate. He appears strong, stable, never rattled by emotions or feelings. He endeavors to dominate and outperform others but does not make it appear that much of an effort. He has relationships with other men built upon respect rather than close, intimate friendship. Intimate relationships are an enigma to him.

Does he sound familiar in part or whole? This describes some men and perhaps reflects a stereotype which is an unfair label. Even though men differ from women, they also differ among themselves.

Our society creates confusion within a man because of the mixed and numerous messages he hears about being a man. Society's expectations for men are often in conflict as are his own expectations of himself.

He is supposed to be "all male" and yet "be a sensitive man." He struggles with being the strong, silent lone wolf vs. being one of the guys; being the family man vs. being independent and always in control; being a handy man vs. being helpless.

As a man develops, he is confronted with his own personal expectations which he has developed from many sources. But these may not match up to who he is. A man's roles in life carry certain expectations, such as husband, father, son, friend, elder, deacon, professional—and there may be conflicts between some of these. All of us as men have expectations of what we would like to be . . . but we also find inconsistencies between these expectations and what we are actually becoming.

Consider the conflicts expressed in this description:

> Men are raised to take charge,
> but they cannot all be their own bosses.
> Men are raised to be primary providers,
> but they find they are now living during
> inflation and recession.
> Men are raised to focus on achievement,
> but success is usually a momentary experience.
> Men are raised to stand on their own,
> but they need support systems.

Men are raised to express "strong" emotions,
   but they often feel "weak" ones like fear and
   sadness too.
Men are raised to be team players,
   but it's often "every man for himself."
Men are raised to be Daddy's Big Boy,
   but expected to remain Mommy's Little Man.
Men are raised to be independent,
   but urged to bond and nest.
Men are raised to follow their dreams,
   but required to be realistic about security.[2]

Women Bend but Men Break

The so-called strength of men is sometimes brittle: women bend but men break. Men and women have a blueprint for their masculinity and femininity but man's blueprint often leads to self-destruction. The pressures to perform, dominate, be strong and prove oneself become very costly.

Many men base their lives on what their minds are telling them they should be. They constantly attempt to live up to their image of masculinity.

The way a man defines masculinity influences how worthwhile he feels as a man. Feelings of masculinity are at the heart of a person's self-concept. If the definition of masculinity is narrow, the person has a very restricted standard for self-worth. If the definition is broad, the man has much more freedom to attain his self-worth. But too many choose the narrow approach. To feel secure, many men need a clear, definite distinction between what is masculine and what is feminine.

What is a typical image of masculinity? Whether we admit it or not, the image appears to be a reaction to what is or has been considered feminine. Here are a few characteristics.

Images of Masculinity

Masculinity traditionally has meant limiting emotional expression and repressing your emotions if you want to be a real man. Who cares about the stress, psychosomatic ailments and potential for a midlife explosion that may be the result! If he violates this image of always being in control of his emotions by having an emotional outburst because his dinner is late, the man will deny the accusation that he is behaving like a spoiled child. He may even yell, "I'm not angry and I am in control!"

Unrestrained sexual conquest is a characteristic of the "real macho" male. Women are sexual trophies to be obtained by conquest. Men who follow this pattern brag about their seductions and endeavor to outdo one another in terms of the quantity of women and even the number of sexual acts in one night.

For the "macho man," fighting is a basic criterion for being masculine. "If you don't fight, you're not much of a man." Fighting personally or being a participant at a violent brawling sports activity establishes his "macho" image.

Vicarious Manhood

The sports arena is a place where millions of men vicariously live out their masculinity. They identify with the players and even though they are sitting in the stands or in front of the TV at home or in a bar, you will hear more expression of feelings and often observe more expressed energy than at any other time. Time and again you will see compulsion to prove oneself. A football player is knocked senseless. A few quiet seconds go by and he gets to his feet a bit shaken. The trainer tries to lead him from the field but he shakes his head and declines. The crowd roars its approval of staying in the game in spite of the pain, once again proving to the world that he is a man. Many former athletes share their permanent injuries with others like an ex-soldier showing his wounds and the purple hearts he received for each one. They brag about these rather than complain because a real man does not complain. You take it in silence "like a man."

Pain is a part of life which you just override. Never give in to pain. Athletes often cripple their careers by continuing to play with an injury, and too often those around the man give him positive reinforcement for continuing to forge ahead with pain. Manliness is equated with enduring pain and it has to be extreme before men give in. They often equate giving in to pain as feminine. Even television commercials show more women than men in need of and using the advertised health products. Men tend not to take care of themselves as well and they are genetically more susceptible to disease. Perhaps that is why some men are lacking in sympathy when others in their family experience pain.

Being *independent* is viewed as masculine and dependency as feminine. Letting others take care of you, whether it be for illness or any other reason, is unacceptable. As we'll see later on, there are exceptions. If a man can stand alone, be self-reliant, express few or no needs, then he is a real "man."

A characteristic very akin to this one is the tendency *not to ask for help.* "I can do it myself! I can figure it out myself! I can learn it myself!" A man can be sick and nobody knows. A man can be lost and everybody knows it, but he still won't stop to ask directions. He will deny that he is lost and mumble something about, "I'm just taking a new way, that's all," turn up the radio and drive faster.

Even in counseling situations, men hesitate to go for help until a major disaster or crisis has occurred.

In our society, *touching* generally is seen as feminine and the majority of men touch very little except for a handshake. Any touching must have a clear-cut, definite purpose.

The Drive to Dominate

For many men winning is tied to their identity. Even Christian men have a strong desire to succeed and win. For many, it is their way of proving their masculine power. And this is the problem . . . that winning equals being masculine or manly. Christian men want to win for God and for themselves. Sometimes the motives are right and other times distorted. Sometimes winning includes dominating or controlling others at all cost.

This drive to dominate others is even reflected in men's preferences for pets. Men tend to prefer dogs rather than cats. Why? Men like the loyalty and obedience of dogs. They can train a dog to obey their every command. Dogs give back love and devotion at all times, not just when they want to eat. You can get a dog to respond at any time, but just try it on a cat!

Cats are much more independent and whether men like to admit it or not, there is a definite power struggle in operation between them and cats!

Cats won't take the rough-housing and abuse a dog will accept. A man says, "Cat! Come here!" and the cat acts as though nothing was said. But dogs obey. If you could listen to conversations between a man and his dog and a man and a cat you would note a difference. Men can be gruff and loud with their dogs but there is still a strong bond of affection between them. Sarcasm often denotes the comments made to cats like, "How would you like to go for a swim today, cat?" or "Well, how many hours are you going to sleep today, you no-good food machine!" Have you ever seen a man launch a dog through the air to see if it would land on all four feet?

The struggle between men and cats is a simple reflection of their need for control.

How do the men in your life handle losing? For some men, losing is a disaster which clouds their entire day or week, and this can include seeing their favorite team lose on TV!

Some men sulk for days and others move into a quiet rage whereby every family member—including the pets—exists quietly until the storm passes. Some men "split." They leave town for a "mini" getaway to recoup. Some men gorge to help themselves feel better. Some men take it out on others—wife, children, business associates, other drivers on the freeway.

Always having to win reveals an unrealistic view of life and a tenuous basis for identity.

The Total Man

A mistake which men make is the false notion that they have to become "totally male" rather than a "whole man." A whole man recognizes and accepts the balance of his life which involves being active and passive, accepting winning and losing, being aggressive and receptive, and accepting the combination of "masculine and feminine" traits that we all have.

A masculine man is a *provider,* not only for himself but for his family. How well he fills that role determines his status as a man. The traditional definition also emphasizes the man's leadership role in the family. But leadership means something today much different than what it meant many years ago. And its meaning does vary from culture to culture. However, many men do gauge their self-worth on how well they provide leadership at home.

The *division of labor* in a marriage or family is also a reflection of masculinity. The male has something to contribute which the woman cannot supply—and these sex roles are also important in fulfilling self-worth. If a man does something considered "masculine" he then fits the male image. But today there is tremendous flexibility and change in these areas. There is more emphasis today on the new role of the father and his unique contribution—and this is a positive change.

One major factor that contributes to a man's feelings of masculinity is his *work*. This is the crucial part of his feelings of masculine security. In most cultures he needs a job to affirm his masculinity. Often women reinforce this to some degree when they are attracted to a man based upon his achievements and even his type of work. Work does provide an outlet for a man's creative and aggressive energies. His work and profession are the cornerstone of his male ego. Masculine rewards are derived from working and achievement, but too often this is taken too far and becomes the only source of satisfaction. This attitude provides a foundation of sand for a man may lose his job, become too old to perform or have an accident. When the job goes, so does the self-esteem and feelings of being a man. There has to be a better basis for self-worth and there is![3]

"The man who is obsessed with work, with meeting responsibilities, who drives himself to an early demise after procreating, making money, possibly becoming successful or powerful (most men never do), has lived his life as a sleepwalker in harness. He has equated the compulsively driven need to live up to the masculine imperative with a 'meaningful' life."[4]

A classic illustration of this is the story of a forty-nine-year-old millionaire who made his money in the electronics field. In three years he developed a twenty-five million-dollar-a-year business. One of his friends had a heart attack while driving a car and a neighbor had open-heart surgery. This prompted our millionaire to have a physical whereupon he discovered that his heart had extensive blockages in the arteries and without an operation he might live for only another fifteen months. He underwent a nine-hour operation. After eight days he was released from the hospital and directed his wife to take him to the office rather than home. Later he said, "And now I'm back on the merry-go-round, working harder, longer hours. Traveling more. More stress. More strain. This is just what I shouldn't be doing after my open-heart surgery. But it doesn't seem to be affecting me. I stop every once in a while and say, 'Why am I pushing myself so hard?' And I say, 'Why not? I feel great.'"[5]

For a man there is a relationship between being autonomous, fearlessly overcoming obstacles, always in control, and being masculine. For some men there is a driving need to be all of these things. This drive overrides common sense and self-care and leads to destructive behavior. I don't know how many times I have heard men say, "Yeah, I know I need to slow down, but . . ." And with many it takes a radical crisis for a change in behavior to occur.

The Masculine Model

Here is where men and women differ. Men are more rigid and compulsively defensive whereas women are more fluid and in touch with reality. Why? A woman has a greater ability to express strength or weakness, dependency or independence, passivity or dominance, emotionality or rationality, courage or fear without any of these being a threat to her self-image. Not so with a man![6]

The more entrenched a man is in this male model, the greater his fear that he might not be masculine enough. Herb Goldberg described this so beautifully: A man represses certain parts of himself because it is not masculine in his eyes. But the repressed part lives on within him. "This repressed core is composed of the man's 'forbidden' parts; his dependency craving, his vulnerability, fear and other emotions, his desire to let go and be taken care of and anything else inside him that might be equated with femininity or unmasculine behavior. The more powerful and threatening this core is, the more rigid the defenses against it will be and the more he will need constantly to prove his autonomy, ability to perform, rationality, unemotionality, lack of dependence, hunger and other human needs."[7]

A worthy goal for a man, which may run counter to his early learning, is to become a "balanced man." And that is where Christianity comes in by eliminating a man's inner conflicts and bringing about this balance as seen in Jesus Christ.

Jesus' personality had several facets, but he did not hide them from anyone. He could chase the corrupters out of his temple in righteous anger, displaying his manhood in what might be called "masculine" ways—and yet later he wept over Jerusalem, displaying what is considered a "feminine" side.

He met the challenge of the enemy and faced them in open debate; and yet he could hold children on his knees and in a moment of tenderness express how precious they were to him and to the kingdom of God.

He walked the bloody highways of Palestine, littered with the flotsam of man's inhumanity to man, pursued, harassed and carrying a price on his head; and yet he could sit and allow a woman to wash his feet and dry them with her hair and rebuke those who thought it inappropriate.

On more than one occasion, he lashed out with a sharp verbal lance, even calling the religious leaders a bunch of "vipers," thus taking the wind right out of them and leaving them dumbfounded; and yet he dealt mercifully with a frantic father who honestly confessed his inability to believe that Jesus could heal his son, touching the boy in tenderness, compassion and power—making him whole.

He had all the legions of heaven on his side and could have, in one master stroke of his manliness, wiped out his enemies. Yet he stood mute before the Roman court, refusing to give dignity to a mob.

Here is the Son of God, Jesus, the Man, who was not asexual, but who never used his sexuality to prove his manhood.

Here is the king of the universe, sweating blood during the deep revulsion he felt in Gethsemane concerning the death that faced him, and yet pressing on to take that death on the cross without wilting.

There is no greater picture of the "whole man"—a man

who was "masculine" in terms of strength, muscle, sinew and courage and yet was not ashamed to show his "feminine" side in terms of tears, compassion, gentleness and peace. He said, "I must finish the task," which in essence means, "I must win for humanity the redemption God designed through me." He won that redemption in the end on the strength of his total manhood, which was beautiful, dynamic and sensitive.[8]

These differences between men and women matter! Men and women were created by God for one another. They are meant to be together, to love one another and live in harmony together. But how can they when they are so different? It's not difficult. You must understand the differences and react and respond accordingly. I don't mean by manipulating or coercing but by being open, honest, confrontive and caring.

If you would like to understand and relate to men—and allow them to be who they are to their fullest potential—ask yourself these questions:

1. What are my beliefs and stereotypes about men?
2. Do my beliefs and stereotypes limit me in allowing men to be different and unique?
3. Do I respond to men in a way which perpetuates behavior on their part that reinforces my view of them?
4. Do I respond in any way that limits my growth and development as a woman?
5. Do I in any way reinforce men's tendency to use work as their source of identity?
6. If the man in your life has a relationship type or work style that bothers you, do you in any way tend to reinforce that style?
7. In any way do you suppress your own identity, assertiveness or sexuality in your relationship with your man?
8. Are you willing to upset the balance and equilibrium in a relationship with a man and create a crisis in order to bring about positive change? Growth does not usually occur for a man without some crisis to create introspection and progress.
9. Do you make it clear in your relationships with men that it is safe for them to be open and honest about their feelings and with you?

10. Are you disconnected from the influence of men in your past so that you are free to develop in your relationship at this time?

Consider these questions by yourself and then discuss them with other women. See what you can learn about yourself (this is a step in understanding a man).

What are the expectations you have for the men in your life? For dad, husband, friends, business associates, son? Do you speak them outwardly or inwardly? Are they realistic or unattainable? How do you handle those needs that are unmet? Many expectations are desires rather than necessities. A tremendous conflict occurs between men and women, when unfulfilled expectations become demands! Married couples, business associates as well as parents succumb to this pattern. Expectations turn into demands which become "oughts and shoulds"—and none of us likes or responds well to demands.

A mother can improve her relationship with her son, a daughter can improve her relationship with her father, a wife can improve her relationship with her husband, if . . . . If what? If you understand why men behave the way they do, what they fear, how they think, what they want, how they perceive life, themselves, women, what motivates them, why they are incapable of responding as women do, how they feel, what gives them security . . . you will be able to relate to them in a much more fulfilling way.

2

Why Is He That Way?

The four women sat together at a table in the dining room of the conference grounds. They had been invited to a large weekend gathering of women to speak on the topic, "How to relate to the man in your life." One series of workshops had concluded and they were evaluating the sessions, discussing also what they would cover in the next series. Most of the women in attendance had come with the desire to develop a better understanding of men in general. But another major question continued to emerge in each of the workshops. Listen to the conversation between the four leaders:

Jan: "It seems that our sessions were well received based on the feedback and response."

Betty: "I think you're right. But how can we address the questions which kept coming up again and again in my workshop?"

Heather: "I had a lot of questions too and they were all centered around the same theme . . . ."

Phyllis interrupted: "By any chance was the question, 'Why are men the way they are? Why do they respond the way they do?'"

They all looked at each other and laughed. Each one had been hearing the same question in each of their sessions.

Jan: "Well, we all have the same question. But how do we answer it? Let's take a few minutes and see what *we* think first of all and then attempt to give some explanation."

And so for the next fifteen minutes they threw around idea after idea. Some of them were:

"God created men the way they are, and women the way they are. That's all."

"It's their genes and hormones that make them the way they are."

"A man's neurological structure is different. It's weird."

"Their birth order makes all the difference. It's their family position."

"Their brains are different and they develop differently."

"Men are just born lacking in emotions."

"It's the way they were raised."

"Their culture conditions determine what they're like."

"It's their toilet training."

"It depends whether they were raised by their father or their mother."

The list could go on and on. But what is the real answer? Why are men the way they are? Why do they respond the way they do? Or are there any answers? How will it help one to understand them? Why?

Is there an unsolvable mystery about the cause of a man's unique qualities, characteristics and quirks? Not really. There are some answers. Some are genetic and hereditary and some are environmental and cultural.

I once heard the statement made, "We are born male and female and raised and trained to be masculine and feminine." Is this statement really true? Is this what you believe? Let's consider some evidence.

A man and a woman think differently. Why? Because their brains are different. No, I don't mean that a man's brain is larger than a woman's! There is a "his" brain and a "her" brain.

The Brain Has Two Sides

If you and I could enter the classroom of a medical school, we would find skeletons and intricately constructed models of body parts. There would be a model of a brain and as we looked at it we would discover that the brain is divided into left and right hemispheres. Your brain is and so is mine. These are connected by nerve fibers. And the two portions each have their own tasks and assignments. If you are sitting down right now, lift your right foot off the floor. Which side of your brain controlled that function? Your left side. And the right side of your brain controls lifting your left foot off the floor.

These two different sides of the brain have more to do than just control our movements. They are the culprits who determine the way we think. Each is quite specialized. Part of the brain is verbal. (I have heard some spouses complain that their mate's entire brain is verbal!) The left hemisphere controls language and reading skills. It gathers up information and processes it logically in a step-by-step fashion. When is the left brain used? Every day when you read a book or article, play a game, sing, write, balance your checkbook and weigh the advantages and disadvantages of buying an item on time versus paying cash.

If you are planning your day's schedule, you may tell yourself that it would be a good idea to leave ten minutes early to drop off the videotape you rented the night before. And you will have planned which street to take so that you will not end up on the wrong side of the street since you want to park right in front of the store. How did you make these decisions? By using the left portion of your brain. It wants to keep your life and mine sensible, organized and on schedule.

And then we have the right side of the brain. That portion of your brain comes into play when you work a jigsaw puzzle, look at a road map, design a new office, plan a room arrangement, solve a geometrical problem or listen to musical selections on the stereo. The right half of your brain does *not* process information step by step like the left portion. Instead, it processes patterns of information. It plays host to our emotions. It has been called the intuitive side of the brain. It will link facts together and come up with a concept. It looks at the whole situation and, as though by magic, the solution appears.

The thinking pattern of the left side of your brain is positive, analytical, linear, explicit, sequential, verbal, concrete, rational and goal-oriented. The right side is intuitive, spontaneous, emotional, nonverbal, visual, artistic, playful, holistic and physical.

If you are more right-side oriented and your man is left-side oriented, how will you communicate? It's as though you each speak a different language! Think about a solution to that problem (if you're right-brain dominant).

Have you ever been in a setting where the speaker focused on dry, detailed facts? Because he was inflexible he was annoyed by interruptions to his train of thought and thus would return to the beginning and review after each distraction. The speaking was monotonous and step by step with little emotional expression. If so, you were listening to a person who was an extreme left-brain dominant.

If you listen to a speaker or someone else in a conversation and they ramble from topic to topic, rely on their own opinion and feelings, are easily led away from the point, may leave gaps in their presentation to give the conclusion, use emotional language and hunches—you are in the presence of the extreme right-brain dominant. The left side wants to know, "What's the bottom line?" and the right side travels around the barn a few times to get there.

Remember when you were in school? You probably ran into individuals who excelled in math or reading but flunked playground! Why? They were functioning with a highly advanced left brain but the right brain was less developed. We shift back and forth between these two sides of the brain as we carry on our daily activities. Here is a man who is a highly proficient chemist, but he also enjoys social activities and goes out dancing twice a week. Which portion of his brain is he using for these tasks? He is using the left side for his work and is careful, accurate and logical. But when he is out dancing, he feels the steps by shifting to the right side of his brain. The chemist may be more comfortable using his left side but is able to make the switch for some right-brain activities.

Recently I was driving in the desert to the High Sierra region of California. As I drove I was looking forward to a good time fishing. I could actually see Walker Lake in my mind and feel the warm sunshine and light, cool breezes. I could also feel the tug on the line from an inquisitive trout. All of a sudden someone passed me doing eighty miles an hour and cut back in, far too close to the front of my car. I was brought back to reality and hit my brakes to make sure I didn't hit him in case he slowed down too rapidly. At that time I moved from my right brain to my left brain. My right brain shifted from the delights of the lake and forest to the left brain which dealt with the traffic problem before me.

Some men make dramatic shifts during their lifetimes from the use of one side of the brain to the other. Such a man was the French postimpressionist painter, Paul Gauguin. A highly successful banker, at the age of thirty-five he left his life in France and went to the South Pacific to paint. His definite and abrupt change is a classic example of the brain organization of males—a high level of lateralization. Men tend to shift farther left or right than women do.

Is there a genetic right-brain/left-brain difference between men and women? Yes. This *is* part of the answer as to why men are the way they are. At birth the cortex of the brain is more highly developed in women than in men. As infants women respond more to the sound of the human voice than do men. Women are left-brain oriented and tend to be more verbally skilled. Men are not. A woman's left brain develops earlier than a man's (this gives her an edge in writing and reading). This is why many little boys do not read or write as well as little girls. A boy can build a complicated model but cannot read as well as the girl who is a year younger. The male's right brain develops earlier than the female's and all through life men tend to use this side of their brain more skillfully in the spatial area.

A man uses the right side of his brain more efficiently than women. And his brain is more highly specialized. If I am a typical man, I will use the left side of my brain for verbal problems and the right side for spatial. If I am putting together a new barbecue grill which came in pieces, I use my right brain to visualize the end result. Thus I shift from one side to the other. I am seeing how it fits together in my mind. If my wife Joyce comes out to discuss who we are having over for dinner, I am responding out of my verbal side, the left.

Personally, I feel that we men do not use all the abilities of the right side as well as we could. The emotional, intuitive side in men is often stunted, partly due to the lack of socialization training and encouragement and partly because of our tendency to use one side of the brain or the other but not so much together.

But a woman is different in the way she uses her brain. And it gives her an advantage over men! A woman's brain is not specialized. It operates wholistically. A man shifts back and forth between the sides of his brain. He can give more focused attention to what he is doing. But a woman uses both sides of her brain simultaneously to work on a problem. The two parts work in cooperation. Why? Because some of the left-brain abilities are duplicated in her right brain and some of the right brain in the left. Women have larger connectors between the two sides even as infants and thus can integrate information more skillfully. They can tune in to everything going on around them. A wife may be handling five hectic activities at one time while her husband is reading a magazine, totally oblivious to the various problems going on right under his nose.

The result causes women to be more perceptive about people than men. Women have greater ability to pick up feelings and sense the difference between what people say and what they mean. This means a woman's expectation of a man's perceptual ability should be tempered with such knowledge.

This is why a woman may recover some of her functions following a stroke whereas a man is limited. Her ability to use both sides means that the undamaged side can step in and begin to fill the void left by the other.

Both men and women have a tendency to prefer one side of the brain or the other, and this does affect our approach to life and work. We do not change our preference or dominance throughout our lifetime, but we can develop the skills of the less-preferred side of our brain. And remember, our culture tends to reinforce these bents and inclinations.[1]

Three Types of Men

Let's consider an example of three types of men who are known to many Americans. For years, many of us listened and reacted to one of America's most famous sports announcers, Howard Cosell. He was an articulate, logical, concise announcer who analyzed each play and was also quite opinionated. Since he was a former lawyer, it was difficult for anyone to argue with him. He was a strong left-brain male.

But he had a sidekick by the name of Don Meredith who was the color commentator. Don would tell warm and humorous stories about his own career. He shared his hunches and described how it felt to be involved in some of the described plays. Don would kid and joke around and was very personable. He functioned out of the right side of his brain.

A third member of the team was Frank Gifford who was a combination of both. Frank had an articulate, interesting style to which almost everyone responded favorably. He was a former professional running back (a position which would involve the right brain), but also graduated with honors from college. He combined verbal skills with feelings, using two well-developed sides of his brain in his presentations.[2]

It is possible for a man or woman to develop the skill of using the least dominant side. An excellent resource on this subject is the book, *Whole Brain Thinking,* by Jacquelyn Wonder and Priscilla Donovan (Ballantine Books).

Birth Order

What accounts for the dominant/passive differences between men? Why are some leaders and others followers? Why are some neat and others sloppy? Here is one approach you can take to answer these questions. Look at the man in your life. If you don't already know the answer, ask him, "What was your birth order in your family? Were you the first, second or last-born?" The answers will explain some of his tendencies.

And now that we've answered this issue, let's move on.

"Not so fast, Norm," you say. "It hasn't been answered for me! Explain. I need more information. You're answering like so many men do . . . not giving any details!"

You're so right. Allow me, please, to elaborate. The main point is—*In all families, a person's birth order, whether male or female, has a lifelong effect on who and what that person turns out to be.* Birth order helps make us unique. It interacts with temperament and parental relationships to shape the man. His rank in his own family birth order helps determine the roles he feels comfortable with as an adult. Birth order can also affect our self-image, what we think of ourselves, how we respond to authority, and how we react to life's circumstances.

The Firstborn

Let me describe the firstborn male for you. While I'm doing this, consider the question: What is it like to be married to a firstborn male or work for one? What can you expect?

Mr. Firstborn is quite easy to identify. This type of person is often the achiever in his respective field. He is the one driven toward success. All seven astronauts in the original Mercury program were firstborns. Firstborns are more highly motivated to achieve than their younger brothers and sisters. It's also interesting to note that magazine and newspaper reporters tend to be firstborns. Since firstborns like structure and order they tend to enter professions which are exacting.

Mr. Firstborn is an experiment for the parents. They anticipate the first child's birth with anxiety and excitement. They learn parenting by "experimenting" on the first child. He (or she) bears the brunt of the parent's discipline and expectations. Instead of letting him develop at his own pace, most mothers work hard to see that he sits and stands and walks and talks and is potty trained at the proper age or even before. The eager parents want to do the task of parenting better than anyone ever did before, and thus the firstborn bears the brunt of all their inexperience, high hopes and enthusiasm. Is it any wonder that achievement becomes a way of life for this fellow? Achievements are valued more than people. Often this man grows up feeling he has to produce or else—and research indicates that firstborns do walk and talk earlier than later siblings. This child receives encouragement, prodding and coaching from parents and grandparents alike. Everyone overparents. Unlike his later brothers and sisters, he has only his parents as models and tends to imitate adult behavior more closely.

Even firstborn girls are pressured to produce and wind up being in charge of the younger brothers and sisters. Mothers have been known to take advantage of them and it's not uncommon for them to earn labels like "the warden," "little mother" or "mother hen."

Firstborns tend to grow up fast and they feel the pressure of the adults around them. When the parents are gone, does the pressure vanish? No. The firstborn continues putting pressure on himself. Firstborns are serious, conscientious, have strong powers of concentration, are list-makers, critical, perfectionistic, goal-oriented achievers. They believe in authority, may be legalistic, are loyal and self-reliant. Don't expect them to come up with many surprises.

This doesn't mean that every firstborn turns out identically. There are no clones. Actually there are two basic types: strong-willed and aggressive or compliant and wanting to please. The first can develop traits that make them the high achievers and hard drivers with lofty expectations and a need to be at the top. Compliant persons strive to please others and usually are very reliable workers. They feast at the table of approval.

How do others respond to the firstborn? Always in a positive way? Not quite.[3]

It used to be, among the Ugandans in East Africa, if the first child was a boy, he was killed immediately. The people believed that if allowed to live he would take his father's strength, absorb his father's spirit and thus bring about the father's demise. They also believed that the father was born again in this son and thus both could not survive.[4]

But the Jewish people in the Old Testament were just the opposite. The first male child was redeemed by special sacrifice at the temple and then enjoyed a privileged place. He received his father's chief blessing and a double portion of the inheritance, became the priest in his household and upon his father's death, the patriarch of the family.

Based upon these examples, how would you like to respond to the firstborn men you know? Bless them according to the Jewish tradition or . . . ?

What happens if two firstborns marry? Look at the list again. What happens if two firstborns have any type of relationship, from marriage to work? Two perfectionists may get along if their standards, timing and behavior are identical and perfect. But if they aren't, watch out! (For information on reducing perfectionistic tendencies, see Chapter 7 of my book, *Making Peace with Your Past.*)

If a firstborn had younger brothers but no sisters, be aware of the fact that he will expect the most from a woman without offering much in return. Not that sure of how to act around women, he has to learn by trial and error. He may be very particular about what he wants in a wife and often has a difficult time making a decision. If he marries a woman who is the oldest of sisters, sparks will ignite in their marriage. They have little experience with the opposite sex and are both used to leadership roles. That could also be true of a marriage with a woman who is a firstborn with younger brothers. Many firstborn males tend to marry lastborn women with older brothers—and they both know their roles quite well. If you find a firstborn with younger sisters you have probably found a man who knows how to treat women well. They often tend to arrange their lives around the needs and desires of their women.

The Secondborn

How many secondborn men do you know? Or do you know how to identify them?

A second or middle child is difficult to describe or even generalize about. When a secondborn child comes into the family, whether male or female, his or her lifestyle is determined by his perception since he plays off the firstborn. He often tends to be the opposite of the firstborn. This person may end up either antagonistic or a pleasant pleaser. He could be a controller or manipulator, a victim or martyr. As a child it is difficult to predict how he will turn out since he tends to bounce off the firstborn. Often a secondborn tries to discover the weaknesses of the firstborn and compete in these areas.

You may see one secondborn who is placid and easygoing and the other hyperactive and pushy. Both have the same root cause. Their perception of the "pacemaker"—the first child—determines the direction they take. If a second child sees the firstborn as unbeatable, he becomes discouraged and gives up competing. From all outward appearances, he becomes easygoing and placid. Or his position could lead to rebellion and delinquency. But if the secondborn feels he or she can overtake the firstborn, watch out for the competition![5]

Perhaps looking at an adult second child can tell you a lot about the firstborn. This person has often been called the mystery child.[6]

Middleborn children tend not to have as many problems or hangups as the firstborn or only children. They tend to be less fearful and anxious than firstborns. Studies show that a middle child tends to be the most secretive of all birth orders. This happens because he feels he didn't receive as much attention as the other children and tends not to confide in others. If this is true, how does this affect you if you are married to such an individual? Perhaps the communication is a bit lacking. This tendency also carries through in the arena of seeking help. The desire to be tough and independent can lead to the entrenchment of problems because the person will not seek assistance from ministers or counselors when needed.

Middle children like to have a lot of friends outside of the family and tend to run with the pack as a child. They are more susceptible to influences such as peer pressure or temperament than others. A plus factor is that middleborns tend to stay married more than all birth orders. They often feel they didn't fit too well in their own family so they are determined to make their new family work.[7]

Some of the other characteristics of the second or middleborn include being a mediator, a maverick, having the fewest photos in the family album, being very loyal to the peer group and having many friends. Parents tend to "let up" on the second child. This may seem like rejection. He usually receives less time and attention than the firstborn. But there are some advantages, as psychologist Kathy Nessel states: "Middle children are tenacious adults because they are used to life being rather unfair. Their expectations are lower, consequently they are more accepting in a relationship. The middle child may say, 'Well, this isn't perfect, but it is kind of nice.' We are not as driven as firstborns, but then again neither are we as compulsive."[8]

By the way, what happens if a secondborn woman and a secondborn man marry? Trouble potential! Why? Even though a middle child can go in many directions, he tends to mediate, negotiate and compromise, which is very positive. But this also means he likes peace at any price. This can turn him into an avoider. And two avoiders in a marriage may end up with a peaceful-looking marriage but underneath all that calm is a raging storm, for communication is nonexistent!

The Lastborn

What about the lastborn or the baby of the family? What is this person like? If he is suppressed by others in the family, he may tend to have low self-esteem. But if he is encouraged and affirmed by others, he will have a strong and healthy self-concept. The family's attitude toward this person is especially important. If you have a relationship with a lastborn, try to discover the family's response to this child. Lastborns tend to receive less discipline than the others, especially from the father, and they are usually spared the pressure of achieving. They are usually quite comfortable in social situations. A pioneer in child development, Dr. Rudolf Dreikurs, commented that, "The youngest child resembles an only child in many respects; but in others his position corresponds to that of the second born, and accordingly he develops a considerable urge to put himself forward. His efforts to outdo all the other children may be remarkably successful. Since he has to use a whole bagful of tricks to mask his situation as the smallest of the family, he often becomes quite inventive and adroit."[9]

Lastborns can end up being the "Baby Boss." They may also be manipulative, charming or show-offs. A lastborn may turn out to be a people person, a good salesperson, precocious and tend to blame others.[10] They may also tend to act the part of the clown. Taking responsibility for oneself may not be that easy. Their charm may get old after awhile. A woman may be drawn to the man's delightful charm and personality while dating, but upon getting married may be furious with his irresponsibility and excessive clowning. As with any type of relationship, adjustments and growth have to occur!

Who comes to mind in the Bible when you think of the lastborn? David was one of those individuals. Cheerful and optimistic as a teenager, he confronted Goliath with confidence. He had a childlike faith that God would take care of him no matter how bad a situation looked. Years later he got into difficulty through murder and adultery. Experiencing repentance, he sought God's forgiveness and then came back to his cheerful and optimistic self. That would be difficult for a firstborn because many of them would tend to hang onto their grief and guilt.

The Only Child

How about one more—the only child! This individual can resemble both the firstborn and the last child. The only child is likely to be achievement-oriented and he often has a high desire to please his parents. He has a position of safety in that he doesn't have to fear being dethroned by any younger brothers or sisters. There may be a tendency for the only child to grow up feeling that life should revolve around him. Why? In many cases the lives of both parents revolved around the child.

Many "onlies" believe that the sole task of their parents is to serve them and their needs. Their feeling of being special could create some difficulties. They often have difficulties developing friendships and because of the lack of siblings do not develop the skills of sharing. They may not have experienced jealousy or competitiveness with others and when confronted with this have difficulty handling it.

Loneliness and protective isolation may become a problem. Many of them state that they would rather be by themselves. An only child may mimic his parents by acting parental but inside may feel like a child. Ambivalence is a part of his life and frequently the only child has a string of broken relationships to contend with throughout life.

Marriage can be an adjustment, especially if there were few dating relationships or friendships growing up. He may look for a wife who can be a mother figure. If a man grew up with several siblings, on the other hand, he learned how to respond to others.

No matter what our birth position, we can change and strengthen the weak areas in our lives. How? Because of the presence of Jesus Christ, our walk through life should be a continual adjustment to others. Again, I would suggest reading my earlier book, *Making Peace with Your Past*.

We haven't fully answered the question asked in this chapter. I'm not sure that it will ever be fully answered. A few ideas were presented here, but others are yet to come. The effect of the father and mother on a man's life awaits you. But before we leave this chapter, why don't you do some investigation yourself? Perhaps you could interview a dozen men and ask them and their spouses or close friends to describe their characteristics. Then ask about their birth order. Chances are, it will fit what we have been talking about.

3

The First Man in Your Life

"How is your heart?" I asked. She looked at me with a quizzical expression on her face.

"My heart? Well, I think it's all right. It's still there and beating! Why would you ask such a question?"

I replied, "Well, let me clarify my question a bit. You and I have been talking about your father for some time. I was just wondering, is your heart open or closed to your father? And, is your father's heart open or closed to you?"

"Why—I've never thought about it in those terms before. Why do you ask?"

"Let me answer your question with another question," I replied. "As you interact with other men in your life, whose face do you see on their faces? Their own or your father's?" A long, stunned silence followed.

The Father's Face

Many women do see their father's face in their husband, friend, boss or even men in general. Why? It happens when a father's love for his daughter is either lacking, lost, fades away or is withdrawn. If the hurt is intense, a woman responds as her father did, by turning off her expression of love for him. Her father's heart is closed to her and her heart is closed to him. Yes, denial often sets in to ease the pain of deficit love. I've heard women say, "I don't need his love or approval." But often there is a lingering secret need for his love and to obtain it she looks to others to fill the void.

Startling? Unusual? Rare? No—common! Yes, all too common.

You've had a relationship with a man—your father. He's had a tremendous impact on your life, in fact, more than you realize. Your history with this man affects your present relationship with other men. Whether he was present or absent, he impacted your life!

What a father *gives* to a daughter can affect her expectations toward other men in her life. What a father *doesn't give* to a daughter can also affect her expectations toward other men.

Understanding what men are like involves understanding your father and your relationship with him. We often make other people into the image of someone in our past and by doing this deny them and us the opportunity to be unique and to change. Do you still respond to other men as you did to your father? Are you an image-maker, or are you now free of your father's hold upon your life? Let's consider the place of Dad in your life.

Most women respond to their fathers through three stages—as a child, as an adolescent and as an adult.

The Father-Daughter Relationship

Think back to when you were a child. How did you and your father interact at that time? What was the picture you had of your father then? How would you describe him? (Try to list ten adjectives describing your father as you saw him when you were a child.)

If your father was somewhat typical he was either in his twenties or thirties when you were a child. But what is a father like with a daughter at that stage? Your father was probably concerned with building his career (and his identity). And this may have been done at the expense of personal time for himself, his marriage, his leisure and friendships. He may have been a working machine. He was striving for the position he would achieve in his forties and fifties.

During this period you may not have seen much of him. In infancy, though, you probably saw enough of him to form an attachment to him. And during your childhood you may have been limited in your time together—or you may have experienced quality time with him because of his business. A contradiction? No. A father may have looked at the time with his daughter as an enjoyable retreat from the pressures of his life. And this may have elicited positive emotions for both of you. Mothers are more involved with their daughters in caretaking and fathers in play. You became his little girl during this time and in most cases Father became your hero.

Frequently mothers are more demanding of their daughters and fathers are tougher on their sons. Attachment to a parent is a normal response in infancy and childhood. A parent supplies our wants and needs and gives us a sense of stability. A childhood pattern may be healthy or painful, but either way it was familiar and familiarity brings security and comfort. Because of childhood attachments, our attraction and attachment to particular people in adulthood can be a carry-over from our past. If our parents were loving, we may be drawn to others similar to our parents.

Janice was a thirty-year-old woman with a dating pattern detrimental to her well-being. She came for counseling because she seemed to be drawn to men who were not really good for her. She even had the insight to realize that she was attracted to flawed men. As we talked, she shared that her father was a very handsome man but also passive and quite ineffective. From early on she had a high admiration for him and tried to deny his weaknesses. But he had disappointed her so many times over the years, she came to feel betrayed by him and resentful. In spite of this experience, she still selected men who were like her father, hoping they would turn out to be dependable.

When you were five or six, and started school, Father may now have added the role of teacher as well as playmate. He may have encouraged you in your schoolwork. The happiness experienced during this decade of life (and especially the earliest years) will form the basis for a woman's security and the way she views and responds to men throughout her life.

Your Father and Your Femininity

If happiness was lacking or deficient in your relationship with this significant man, what is it that suffers? Your femininity! If a father is either absent, rejecting or angry, a girl becomes discouraged in her initial and important interaction with a man. This is a highly impressionable time in her life. If she has no experience in gaining attention from a man, being delighted by a man or being highly prized by or flirting with a man, her development at this point is incomplete and stunted. Fathers do affect their daughters' femininity! A father who is not too frightened of his daughter's sexuality and is warm and accepting is helping the daughter grow and develop in a normal manner. Although a woman's sexuality develops over a lifetime, it is definitely affected by her father. A father's smile when his daughter flirts or bats her eyelashes encourages this behavior. Frowning at this time may encourage her to be reserved. Some fathers encourage the feminine side of their daughters. Others feel threatened by it and so the daughter feels uncomfortable in the male-female relationship of courtship.

A father who is able to admire his daughter's dresses, initial efforts at makeup, jewelry and her attractiveness, helps her develop the confidence she needs in relating to other men in her life. Unfortunately, some fathers are uncomfortable with a daughter's attempts at femininity. They either ridicule her, are absent much of the time or are too tired or irritable to accept her growth. These responses have their effect, too. How? By causing her to be insecure about herself as a woman and her ability to attract a man.

The lack of closeness to an accepting father can leave a woman with a gaping wound. One of the deepest is insecurity. Another wound is detachment because she does not know how to be close to a man and thus feels isolated. Some women learn not to expect love, warmth, closeness or intimacy from a man. Often a woman, who has not been given the legacy of love and attention from her father, is left feeling deeply enraged. And when any man in her life lets her down, the stored-up anger erupts. This can either punish the man in her life or drive him away!

Unfortunately, because of this lack in a woman's development, she may either experience an absence of desire for men in her life—or have an inordinate appetite for them! An excessive hunger may develop which carries with it demands that any man must be totally devoted to her. Any slip is reason enough for her to dismiss him. Anger is her protection. Other women develop an addiction to the excitement and delight of the courtship process and want to stay in this state perpetually.

It is difficult to tolerate the sameness of a long-term routine relationship with any man. Some crave excitement and newness and as it begins to wane, so does their interest in the man. They are addicted and the only antidote is a new man.

Some fathers are just the opposite. They are overbearing and demand too much of their daughters. They need the daughter's admiration and cling too long to the child, stunting her growth and independence. Unfortunately, this makes it difficult for a daughter to leave her father psychologically. She tends to view other men in her life as not measuring up to her own father whom she remembers as interesting, attentive and considerate. If a woman was babied for too long it makes it difficult for other men in her life since they are being compared to an all-giving father. Harsh fathers tend to produce women who are either afraid of men or spend their lives trying to please them. Gentle fathers, on the other hand, can give a daughter the best potential for relationships with men. This, in turn, helps them become successful in careers.

Some fathers can be painfully disappointing to a daughter. If a father is weak and unassertive, he is unavailable for the support and closeness which she needs. A daughter with a weak father may develop a fear of overwhelming him with any kind of strong feelings. She may feel he is incapable of helping her fill her emotional needs. These feelings can lead a daughter to feel like something is wrong with her for wanting more!

A father can show occasional weakness which is understood and accepted because of his other displays of stability and strength. But if a father is consistently a poor provider, is unable to get along with others, undervalues himself, avoids any risks, is wishy-washy, unassertive or ineffectual, a daughter feels cheated. She may either retreat from other men in her life or be demanding with them.

But some fathers are more like tyrannical dictators. They control family members and look on their children as their possessions, treating them accordingly. These men shape the lives of their daughters in a variety of ways. Some daughters decide they are going to "fight this man." But their defiance may lead to punishment which causes either remorse or inward seething. They may be either chastened or glowered at and then the pattern repeats itself. Constant warfare ensues.

Defiance is cultured and developed and unfortunately probably carries over to other men in their lives. Requests are interpreted as demands and any strong man is an invitation to a battle.

Some daughters, however, avoid the conflicts by looking for a man who is passive and compromising. But this man seems unfulfilling, too, because he is so different from the father.

Changing the Pattern

Some women reading this scenario may feel overwhelmed and discouraged. Why? Because it describes their experience. But the effects of childhood experiences are not everlasting! A process which takes consistent effort and healthy discomfort is possible: you can recognize what your father was like and his effect on you and then take the steps necessary to change that pattern.

After childhood a daughter moves into adolescence and her father is in his late thirties or forties. Both of them are asking the same question, "Who am I?" She may be beginning to rebel against authority and conventions, may be moody, restless, asking significant questions about life and concerned about physical changes. Well, so is he! A father has a multitude of questions at this stage, but insufficient time to deal with them. A daughter's growth and changes can add pressure both financially and emotionally.

A daughter sees her father differently now. Why? Because he *is* different and his faults more obvious. She no longer worships him or sees him as a hero. A daughter sees more flaws in her father which may be upsetting—but it is healthy for her to gain a realistic perspective about men. However, if at this time the father makes radical negative changes, such as deserting the family, a daughter may feel that she cannot allow herself to be vulnerable to any man. "Men leave women and it hurts too much," is the attitude which begins to develop. During this time a daughter is beginning the process of emotional separation from her dad. This is a normal part of her development. And there will be some pain and upset, no matter what the relationship.

The personal struggles of a man at this time (about his work, his relationship with his wife, his sexuality, his faith) all affect his relationship with his developing daughter.

A father can handicap his daughter emotionally and sexually at this time by his response to his daughter's developing sexuality. If he is unsettled or threatened by his teenage daughter's development, he may retreat and withdraw from her, leaving parental advice and interaction to the mother. This lack of response and interaction with her father at this time leaves her ill equipped to respond adequately to men romantically. She may end up having difficulty coping with intense feelings which arise from sexual intimacy.

Dr. William S. Appleton says:

> It is the fortunate adolescent girl who has a warm, not seductive, and attentive, not interfering, father who brings reasonable patience to bear upon her rebellion and aggression. When she is fourteen or fifteen she can shout at him "I hate you" and he will not retaliate too angrily or withdraw from her. They both try as well as they can to adjust to her becoming a sexual woman, rather than pretending she is still a little girl. He enjoys seeing her body mature without comment or fear. As he accepts her sexual development, so will she, although both are a little uncomfortable about it. Paternal responsiveness and acceptance help a woman to grow sexually. By trying not to rival her boyfriends, not to be brighter and more attractive than they, but to act the part of father even when it requires stands which are unpopular with her and make her angry, he allows someone to take her away from him.[1]

The problems of a childhood relationship may be perpetuated and reinforced at this time. What does a father experience when his daughter becomes a teenager? It's not an easy time for him. He has to be flexible to deal with an adolescent and this is difficult for him because of his own struggles. A daughter is uncomfortable about her body and her father may be just as uncomfortable. She may be embarrassed at the smallest thing he does or says. She is unpredictable and he wants predictability! He wants to hold on to her but knows he needs to let go. He needs to help her grow independent of him and yet this can leave a void in his life. It is too bad that a father usually doesn't share with his wife and daughter his inner feelings at this time of life. If the entire family were able to work together on these changes, it would be more comfortable for everyone.

A Help or a Hindrance?

A daughter wants to be her own person, but still wants assistance. A father's help is perceived as interference, ordering and babying. He has to find a way to help her even though she often resents his aid. It is not easy to offer advice to a daughter which is ignored and then is interpreted as an attack. If a father is too preoccupied with his career or midlife issues, there is little patience to discuss issues with his daughter. In this case, he may give angry orders. This leads to quarrels or withdrawal on the part of the daughter. There is a contest of wills and conflicts over rules emerge more and more.

Your father was probably like most dads. Part of him wanted you to grow up and be strong, responsible and independent. And part of him wanted you to continue to be dependent and lean on him. In his attempt both to release you and hold on to you he may have given you double messages.

"I'd like you to really get ahead in your career, but you need to listen to what I have to say."

"You know I raised you to make your own decisions, but if you go into that line of work, don't expect any help from me."

"You have good taste, but couldn't you wear something a little more appropriate tonight?"

How do daughters respond? Many work at being noticed by their father if he is absent too much. If he wants to know about her private life, she becomes more reclusive. If he is intolerant of her adolescent behavior or tendencies, she wants respect.

If these issues cannot be worked out and resolved, a woman may tend to repeat her anger and rebellion with men in her adulthood. A positive pattern of growing up and becoming independent takes cooperation between a father and daughter.

The third stage of response between a father and daughter begins when the daughter becomes an adult. When most fathers are in their late forties or fifties, the daughter leaves. If other factors of his life are going well, he is able to handle it, even though there will be some sadness. A psychologically stable father accepts the loss, mourns, recovers and moves into a new phase of his life. Unstable fathers attempt to hold on through manipulation, clinging or even anger. For a woman's development with other men in her life, it is vital that her father encourage and accept her leaving while remaining available if needed. For her to function as an adult with others, he needs to accept her as a mature person himself. It is to be hoped that as she leaves the home, it is as an adult who can confidently care for herself.

Fathers not only affect a daughter's response to men but their careers as well. A selfish father backs only what he wants his daughter to do while a supportive one encourages her to make her own decisions and reinforces those. A warm, supportive father with high expectations often shows his daughter how to enter and be successful in a career. But cold fathers with high expectations and little practical instruction help to create ambitious, frustrated and angry daughters who have difficulty in their careers.

Again, Dr. Appleton points out:

> The resolution within the woman in her twenties of her feelings about the Fall of Father helps her gain control of herself, feel strong, and be able to separate. She has behind her in adolescence the feeling of anger and disappointment toward him which helped her begin to leave him. The process of reconciliation between them releases her feelings. If she continues her adolescent anger toward him throughout her twenties her emotions (in spite of being negative) will continue to be tied up with him. By forgiving him and accepting him with his faults she finds it much easier to leave.[2]

Negative Parental Attitudes

A woman experiences a mixture of feelings at this time. These vary from wanting to rely upon Father but also wanting to separate from him. Some rely too much and some separate too much and both affect the process of healthy separation and mourning. But it is possible for women to handle the pain of separation and move to the adult level, responding to Dad as an adult and to other men in a healthy manner.[3]

Let's go back now and reconsider several of the most common parental attitudes which shape our lives in a negative manner. You may identify with one or more of these, or from what you know, you may realize that the man in your life experienced one of these parental attitudes which will help explain who he is today. You may be a person, however, who comes from a home where you experienced total acceptance and love. If so, praise God for this positive life-shaping experience.

Overcoercion

Some fathers tend to be *overcoercive*. He gave you constant directions, instruction and reminders. If questioned, he would reply with, "I just wanted to make life easier for you." In reality, however, he may have been avoiding the time and effort it takes to help you develop your own independence. This father controlled, shaped and left you little opportunity to become your own person. Pursuing your own interests and inclinations was an illusive dream. You ended up being the puppet on a string, dangling and dancing to the pulls of your director.

As a child you learned a pattern of behavior that even today may be visible in your relationship with other men. As a child you could choose to resist the strong directives and influence (either overtly or covertly) or to submit, follow and learn to rely upon others to live your life for you. How do you resist overcoercion? By forgetting, procrastinating, dawdling or escaping into daydreams. But if you learned to submit, you can easily follow this pattern of needing outside direction even into adulthood and marriage. You may tend to view all men through the filtered glasses of "order givers, directors and controllers."

Some marriages work out when one person is an overcoercer and the other is docile. They work out, but are lacking in intimacy. But what happens if an overcoercive man marries a woman who is definitely not coercive? What if she is very nondemanding—and that is one of the reasons why he was attracted to her! Even if she is nondemanding, she carries certain expectations with her into marriage, such as normal, everyday, common-sense tasks of daily living. Her husband begins to resist these tasks through his typical responses—procrastination, forgetting and neglect. In time, what happens? The nondemanding wife, who at first exerted no pressure, is pushed into a coercive role by her husband's lack of involvement. Now the passive-resister husband has a real person to resist. His attitude helped create a parent from his past!

Oversubmission

What happens to your relationship with men if your parents happened to be *oversubmissive* in their interactions with you? Out of their "love" for a child many parents may oversubmit to a child's demands, temper outbursts or impulsive whims. They end up allowing a child to rule and dictate to the parents! The pattern is set for a child to be demanding with little regard for others. Limits are not learned early in life. This then becomes an adult pattern. Excesses can easily occur in eating, drinking and spending money. Clothes are a favorite form of overindulgence, more so with women than with men. After all, "Who wants to dress out of fashion?" It is difficult for this individual to consider the rights of others. If a woman makes demands on the men in her life, often she ends up being pushed away and then wondering, *Why am I constantly rejected?*

Overindulgence

A somewhat similar parental pattern occurs when parents overindulge the child. *Overindulgence* involves lavishing gifts and privileges upon a child, not because the child wants or requests this attention, but because the parent believes this is necessary. After years and years of this service, a child can become bored, apathetic and lose initiative and spontaneity. He or she fails to learn to work for rewards and has little persistence.

This child turns into an indulged adult who believes other people should cater to her. If this doesn't occur, others are at fault and life becomes an endless search for those who will cater to her.

An overindulged man or woman has an insatiable need for being fulfilled. This person subconsciously sets up a pattern of incessant demanding which leads to dissatisfaction, greed and self-centeredness. Success doesn't satisfy. If eighty percent of an experience was enjoyable, the person focuses upon the remaining twenty percent which was unfulfilling. These people are afraid of being abandoned and because their dependency tends to drain the nourishment from others, in time they drive others away. They develop a unique ability to poison relationships and project the blame on others.

What happens to us in our relationships with others if we were overindulged? I have seen so many couples like this and one of the most frequent results is mirrored in one wife's comment: "Why should I have to tell him what my needs are? We've been married for eight years now and you would think he would know by this time. He should be able to sense what I want. Telling someone takes all the fun and romance out of it!" And the husband is sitting there rolling his eyes and throwing up his hands in exasperation and frustration! Parents read their minds, so why shouldn't others do the same? "Read my mind, anticipate and provide" is life's motto. Life for an indulged woman (or man) is full of shoulds and oughts directed toward other people.

An indulged person lacks in his or her ability to make others feel good. In fact, these people often end up making others feel indebted to them. As one person told me, "My father was one of those overindulged people. For years and years I have tried to satisfy him and it just doesn't work! I make all these efforts to go out of my way to visit and Dad thanks me for coming, but in the same breath tells me I don't come as often as I should. He can never be satisfied. So why try?"

In a relationship, the overindulged person tends not to listen. The other person attempts to make a point, but for some reason, it doesn't register. That is why the same problems and discussions are carried on for years.

In a relationship with an overindulged individual, there are constant demands and expectations operating, but the partner may not even know about all the demands. It is done passively.

Infantile fantasies that have never been resolved present major obstacles to a man/woman relationship—unless the two individuals want a parent/child marriage. Satisfaction may occur if one person wants to fulfill his own needs by indulging the other. But this is not a healthy, balanced relationship. Eventually, the giving person becomes weary of never receiving.

An overindulged person rarely takes initiative, especially in marriage. For example, a husband who was overindulged was incapable of developing a deep, intimate relationship with his wife. Most of his relationships in life were shallow. He was very passive and allowed others to carry the load for him. He didn't have the insight to discover that his unhappiness came from himself rather than being caused by the people around him. He blamed others instead. As I worked with him, I could see the pattern emerging and could actually predict what was going to happen. In his relationships prior to marriage, he was dissatisfied and disappointed. Upon marrying, he thought he had found the ultimate provider. But again, disappointment. In the ensuing years, he repeated this pattern with three other marriage partners, but was never satisfied.

Perfectionism

Some of you came from a home in which love and acceptance was contaminated. It was contaminated because it was conditional. Your father may have demanded *perfection* from you. Your performance had to be above and beyond all normal standards and only then did you experience acceptance, approval and love. And now this pattern affects your response to men and how you view them! This type of parenting produces perfectionists so you constantly try to prove your worth. Perfectionism is a thief because the rewards it offers take away the joy and satisfaction of life for you (and those around you). Demanding perfection of ourselves means that we have assigned our life to a set of rules. Perfectionists live with a list of shoulds, musts and oughts in their mind. "I must be perfect. I must never fail. I must never make a mistake. I must play it safe so I succeed."

The list of beliefs is endless and affects relationships with the men in your life. Being ordinary is an intolerable situation. Everything has to be the best: the party, your man, the way he dresses, the way you have sex, the best behaved children, and the list goes on. Standards set for the man in your life are unattainable and cause discouragement for you and him.

Perfectionists tend to go through life alone. You may tend to work and work, but not ask for help since it's a weakness to request assistance and after all, other people won't do it according to your standard anyway. You may think in "all-or-nothing" terms. "Either I go on a diet and lose it all or nothing." There is no halfway. This is why so many perfectionists are procrastinators. A task has to be done completely and without chance of failure or why try?

And there is only one way to do a task—one correct way. The demands placed on oneself are soon projected onto others and we begin to remold and refashion their lives.

Recently I visited in a home that was a showcase. I mean, it was perfection personified! The furnishings, the decor, the magazines—every item was perfectly arranged. Even the drapes were evenly hung without the slightest sag. To the exact inch, every picture was placed perfectly. You could have taken a tape measure to each one and they would have come out exact. Every magazine was laid out at the proper angle and in perfect sequence. There was nothing irregular in this home except perhaps for the woman who was responsible for the display. From the atmosphere you could tell that the children and husband were uncomfortable in this showcase. It wasn't a home to them, it was a floor display from a department store. In maintaining this dust-free, clutter-free, orderly, sterile showcase, the woman frustrated herself and everyone else.

It was unfortunate that she could not enjoy what she had created. She paid meticulous attention to the details and was very precise in what she did, but it was never enough. It was as though there was a little voice inside her (her father?) saying, "It's not enough. It could be better." And she always felt it could be better. I could compliment her every half hour, but it would never last. She felt like a "successful failure." She had her own marriage and family, but was still trying to please a demanding father whom she still allowed to control her life.

But remember—this pattern can be broken! This endless striving for adequacy is an elusive phantom. Our adequacy has been given to us as a free gift by God himself through the gift of his Son, Jesus Christ. And there is the irony. We strive to attain this when it is already there—given freely. (As I mentioned earlier, this chapter is designed to help identify the issues and not resolve them. To help overcome this pattern and any of the others mentioned, please refer to my book, *Making Peace with Your Past,* where each of these is described in greater detail with practical suggestions to help bring about change.)

Rejection

What about a father who *rejected* you? There are many reasons why rejection occurred, but if it happened to you, it left its brand. Forms of rejection can include belittling statements, never doing enough, being given too much responsibility or being told, "You're worthless." Withholding love and affection convey rejection. Being abused physically or sexually conveys rejection. And what is the result?

Hugh Missildine explains:

> It is difficult to feel at home in the world if you have never felt at home in your own home. If you were rejected as a child, you have an extreme emotional handicap: you are, in effect, the original person "without a country."
>
> You may see yourself as an outlaw, unacceptable to yourself and others. Your self-depreciation is bitter and you feel, almost automatically, bitterness towards others that leads you often to distort the attitudes of others.[4]

Your self-esteem is low. Above everything else, self-image is affected when rejection has been a pattern of our lives. If we were rejected by a father, we tend to reject ourselves since we believe that parent. We become a worse critic than others! We anticipate rejection and read it into other's responses. How does it affect a woman's relationship with a man? A rejected person enters a relationship almost starving for love and acceptance. This leads to further self-rejection!

If, in your relationship, you happen to select a rejected person, watch out! Your expectations and demands of one another can lead you to heights of frustration, disappointment and anger! Your relationship or marriage can be one of constant need for attention, acceptance and affection. If your partner is unable to respond at times with the intensity you expect, the feeling of rejection settles in once again.

Often a rejected individual questions her partner's love. She needs repetitive reassurance. But in time, the partner or spouse will become fed up with being doubted and may say, "You can believe what you want to believe! Either you take what I say at face value, or you don't. I don't have any other way of convincing you, and I am sick and tired of trying! I give up!" And what does this create? More rejection, even though the person's frustration is justified.

Reliving Rejection

The irony of it all is seen when a rejected individual actually seeks out a marriage partner who will repeat what she experienced as a child. She is familiar with the type of mistreatment she received for so many years. When the rejection occurs, she relives her old familiar pattern. Others select partners who are replicas of their rejecting parent and their hope is that this person, in spite of being so similar to their parent, will accept them. If the acceptance occurs, then they can prove that they were not defective as a child but the rejecting parent was the one with the defect. But unfortunately, the one they selected may be like their parent in every way and they end up going to a dry well for water. Many choose to remain rejected people. As Christians we are not rejected people but highly loved and accepted.

For those who discover this and learn to live their lives as accepted persons, it is well worth the effort.[5]

You too may have mixed feelings. Part of you may want to be emotionally free from your father and part of you may want to be emotionally bound. How close are you to your father now? Let's take a look.

Do you live near him and if so, why?
Do you live with him, and if so, why?
What are your expectations for him at this time in your life?
What are his expectations for you at this time in your life?
Describe how you are still dependent upon your father.
Describe how you are independent of your father.
How would you feel if you had less involvement or contact with your father?

In what way are you involved in your father's life at this time?
What is unresolved or unfinished between you and your father?
In what way are the other men in your life similar to or dissimilar from your father? Why is that?
In what way do you still seek the approval of your father?
In what way do you still need the approval of your father?
How do you feel when you experience your father's disapproval?
Do you need to forgive something your father did in the past? If so, what is it? Can you forgive without trying to change him?
Describe the type of love and acceptance you feel from your father.
What specifically did he do to indicate to you that he loved and accepted you?
If you feel unloved and rejected, what is this based upon?

If difficulties and deficits occurred in a woman's relationship with her father, the intellectual awareness of this needs to be converted into emotional knowledge to undo the negative effects of growing up.

What about you? Was the love and acceptance you received early in life sufficient? If you didn't get the positive loving you really needed from your father—and if it is limiting you today in your relationships with others—can the early damage be repaired? Yes! The early wounds no longer have to fester. Healing and growth can occur.

Remember: If you were mistreated, unloved or rejected by your father, it is a statement about him rather than you. It reflects a deficiency in his ability to love and accept rather than a defect in you! And he could have been responding and reacting to his struggles generated from defects in his upbringing. Isn't it about time to break the cycle?

You may have a birth certificate in the drawer showing that you are officially an adult. But an adult is his own person. Many today are limited by their ways of thinking and acting, and so dependent upon other's responses that they really are not their own persons. Howard Halpern said, "We are like a corporation that has gone public and other people own controlling shares. And for many of us in the position, the biggest shareholders are our parents."[6] What about you?

4

The Other Man in Your Man's Life

There is a man in your man's life, too—a very important man who may be directing and influencing your man's life even though he is not aware of it! Most men grow up with unfinished business between themselves and their own fathers. As you have been affected (and perhaps still are) by your father, so have the men in your life been affected by their fathers.

A man's father is the second major relationship in his life. His mother is first and remains primary for several years. But then in time, he gives up his warm, nurturing, caregiving mother for a closer relationship with his father. He switches now from saying, "Hi, Mom" to "Hi, Dad." Father is there to provide a rich model of manhood. But what if he isn't such a good model? Then what happens? A little boy does perceive his father as close and as caring as his mother, but often also experiences him as a distant figure. This is why so many men grow up wounded because they have left the safety and warmth of the mother relationship to discover a father who is remote.

This next statement is strong but nevertheless has to be made: One of the greatest *underestimated* tragedies of our day is the psychological and physical distance of fathers from their children. This distance is contrary to the explicit teaching of scripture which defines the roles and involvement of the father with a child.

It is understandable when a man has a father who is *alive* and inaccessible.

Note some of the findings: A survey of father-child contact after parents divorced showed that by early adolescence 50 percent of the children had *no* contact with their fathers and 30 percent had only *sporadic* contact. Only 20 percent of the children saw their fathers once a week or more.[1]

The Hite survey of 7,239 men indicated that "almost no men said they had been or were close to their fathers."[2] Judith Arcana stated that in her interviews for her work on mothers and sons, only "about one percent of the sons described good relations with their fathers."[3]

A study of 71 male clients by a psychologist focused on the father-son relationship. The results indicated that fathers were physically absent for 23 percent of the time, 29 percent were psychologically absent because of overinvolvement with work, uninterested or passive; 18 percent had psychologically absent fathers who were austere, moralistic and emotionally uninvolved, and 15 percent had fathers who were dangerous and threatening to their sons. Only 15 percent of these cases indicated fathers who had loving, caring involvement with their sons.[4]

The results? Father hunger, a sense of abandonment from mother. She abandoned him to a father who didn't provide the closeness he needed! This leads to the view that women are *supposed* to give warmth, love, care and nurturing which shapes how he views and responds to women in later life. This may be why many men are threatened when their wives (who previously stayed at home) now develop their own careers and are unavailable at night or on weekends. The ancient fear and feelings of abandonment may emerge. This relationship with father can also shape his view of what a man is like and how he behaves: Men are distant and remote and women are the ones who have relationships.

The Wounded Father

Samuel Osherson talks about men carrying with them an image of a wounded father. This picture of Father is a mixture of fantasy and reality. When a father isn't there physically or psychologically, a son has fertile material for mistaken imaginings about his parent. He may idealize and stand in awe of his father or begin to degrade him because of his anger. But if Father is present physically but absent psychologically, a son may see him as angry, passive, distant, rejecting or incompetent. Instead of growing up identifying with a real man and father, he misidentifies with a distant image and fails to develop any type of emotional connection which is so necessary. Therefore, many men grow up seeing their fathers as inadequate, lacking or wounded in some way. According to Osherson, there are many variations of this. Do any of these fit the father of the man in your life?

Some men are seen as the all-suffering father. "Father gave up so much for me since he worked so hard and was away so much." This can lead a man to believe that he must live up to the expectation of his father's sacrifice. He must repay this sacrifice by either achieving so much for his father or being just like him. And if he takes this course, that will affect his relationship with you!

Some fathers are seen as saintly or heroic. Actually, the father's coming and going can be quite exciting to a young boy who idealizes this man and sees him as a hero. Since father had the freedom to come and go as *he* pleased, travel and run his own life, the son may copy this when he has his own family.

Other fathers are discovered to be weak and vulnerable as well as distant. This creates serious consequences. While Father appears successful outside the home, at home he may be dominated and berated by his wife. He may be seen as weak and needy which is uncomfortable to the son. Unfortunately, to understand this distant father he may have to rely upon his mother to explain to him why Dad does what he does. What she says about his father may further shape his view of men. A son may also develop an anger toward women. Why? Because of the anger he has toward his own mother for her attack upon Dad. In fact, many men grow up blaming their mothers for their fathers' lack of involvement with them. How does this affect their relationship with their own wives and women in general? Your answer is probably correct!

Many men have fathers who were angry. Anger is a safe emotion for a man to express. But this anger may be interpreted as rejection and disappointment. Often the relationship between a man and his father creates unrecognized stresses.

Many fathers are seen as strong and powerful. If a young man feels he has surpassed Dad and now has more to offer, this once powerful figure is no longer there to use as a pattern. This brings up feelings of isolation and loneliness.

Some young men continue to compete with their fathers throughout their lives and in so doing never make a mature separation from their fathers. They are still too connected with Dad which influences their lives. I have heard wives complain about the amount of influence Dad has on their husbands. This influence is evident by the man having to: 1) surpass his father; 2) please his father; 3) make his father angry; or 4) depend too much on his father. Are any of these factors affecting the significant men in your life?

The results of any type of incomplete father figure are serious. Few men learn much about their father's inner life. There are so many unasked and unanswered questions which men want answered by their fathers, such as:

Do you feel empty dealing with the uncertainties of being an adult?
What gives you the greatest sense of satisfaction?
What was the saddest time of your life?
What was the happiest time of your life?
What do you wish you could have asked your own father but never did?
What is your greatest achievement and why?
What was your greatest disappointment and why?
How do you feel about dying?
What frightens you the most about dying?
What do you want to be doing when you're 65?
What do you like about women and what don't you like?
If you could tell me something to do as a man that is different from what you did, what would it be?

Has the man in your life asked his father these questions? Ask him. If he hasn't (and the chances are good that he hasn't) ask him how he thinks his father would answer. And then ask him how he personally would answer these questions at this point in his life.

The tragedy of having a father who is absent psychologically is the lack of a male model who is emotionally accessible.

60 ☐ **H. Norman Wright**

The lack of an intimate bond between father and son means a man enters into manhood with a deficit and an inability to relate emotionally. He also maintains a conflicted image of what a man and a father are.[5]

Types of Fathers

In his insightful work, *The Secrets Men Keep,* Dr. Ken Druck describes seven types of fathers and the effects upon their sons.[6] As you read these categories, please ask yourself the following questions:

1. In what way was my father like this and how did this affect my view of men?
2. From my own perspective, in what way is the man in my life's father like this?
3. Would this man describe his own father in this way? How would he say this affected him?

The *Admiral Father* runs and guides the entire family. He wants everything to flow smoothly and is very concerned about his responsibilities. As activities happen in the family, he sees that they run without a hitch, but does not enter in himself. He supervises, disciplines, gives orders and direction and makes sure the fleet is sailing according to the book. He thrives on consistency and predictability—and others must respond as he decides. Life is serious and thus you have to stay in control and be prepared.

What does an Admiral Father give to a son? Respect for authority as well as an oversensitivity to authority. An open or subtle rebellion to authority figures. A dependency on external rules for order and security. A sense of order, discipline and consistency in his life.

What is lacking in this type of relationship? Warmth, affection, closeness, acceptance, intimacy and a model of vulnerability and spontaneity. This can leave a son with a strong need for approval and a lack of understanding of his own individuality and uniqueness.

A question for you the reader: How might a man with this type of father respond to the women in his life? Think about it.

Some fathers fit the category of the *Nice Father.* Others notice and comment upon this. He is so easygoing, agreeable and likable. He is consistent and passive and does not express his inner feelings to anyone. Afraid to risk a deep involvement with others, he is cautious and lacks trust in himself and his inner thoughts and feelings. Because of this nonexpression, he tends to store up hurts and grievances and expresses them either through occasional explosions or through passive-aggressive responses such as forgetting, being late or using silence.

Sons with Nice Fathers have as a legacy: An easygoing style of relating to others on a superficial level. A shallow communication pattern. A cautious, "safe" attitude toward relationships—and limits and boundaries which are fuzzy.

What does a son end up lacking in his life with this pattern? A model for resolving conflicts and assertiveness. The ability to build closeness and depth in relationships.

A question for you the reader: How might a man with this type of father respond to the women in his life? Think about it.

Some fathers are best described as *Professors.* They see their role as a teacher and that is their primary calling in life—to teach their children what is "right." Absolutes are essential. There is right and wrong and black and white—no in-betweens. Every opportunity to lecture is taken and this father delights in revealing his knowledge and other people's ignorance. It doesn't matter if his children or even his wife are embarrassed by his presentation. He is insensitive to the fact that his approach undermines self-confidence and creates distance between himself and others. He doesn't even catch the fact that others no longer listen to him.

The legacy which is left for a son is: Cognitive head information. An ability to tune out others. A feeling that he didn't really count as a real person to Dad. An inward voice which says, "You're not perfect. Shape up." Low self-esteem which is the result of self-doubt.

What is lacking? A son coming from this type of relationship with his father looks for others who will accept and trust him and will relate to him without degrading him. But he also tends to look for others to tell him what to do.

A question for you the reader: How might a man with this type of father respond to the women in his life? Think about it.

The *Angry Martyr Father* is an enigma to his family. Inwardly he is troubled because he does not enjoy his life. But he doesn't share this with others. Instead, he lets it build up and then explodes and dumps his tension, frustration and anger on his family. The family learns to tiptoe around him since they never know when he is going to explode. Often feeling guilty, he may use alcohol to drown his guilt. He lives with a constant inward feeling of being stuck and unhappy. Because they are psychologically absent, many of these fathers eventually leave physically.

The legacy from this father is extensive: He gives his son a model of depression and unhappiness and perhaps guilt. The son wonders, *Was I responsible in some way for Dad's unhappiness?* A son also feels a sense of loss, abandonment and neglect. He may wonder if he was ever wanted by his father. Or he may have to fill in for his father if there are areas of neglect. This creates resentment.

The lack in his life: Thus a son needs to learn a healthy expression of anger and unhappiness rather than following Dad's example and repressing it. He may need to become a "Superdad" to make up for the lack of his own dad. He may have a need to prove that all men (including himself) are no good.

A question for you the reader: How might a man with this type of father respond to the women in his life? Think about it.

The *Hard-working Father* is very common. A devoted provider, he sincerely believes that the way to show love to his family is to give them a good life. He works ten to fifteen hours a day, six days a week, which leaves little space for emotional nourishment or play time at home. Achievement is primary and if stress occurs, he just works harder. He is not seen as a "fun" or "enjoyment-oriented" person. Physical and family problems stemming from this isolation are common. This father is often called "the unknown phantom." He exists but is rarely seen.

His legacy: A model of hard work and the message that work comes first. A father who is stress-prone which can lead to an early death. A son may feel cheated by this. Guilt may occur when the son is having fun or on vacation. He envisions Dad looking over his shoulder and saying, "You should be working. Work first and then play if there is time!"

What is lacking? The son of this father has several deficits: He wonders what it would be like to have a balanced father—one who provides a model of how to use personal time. What is a close, intimate family like? What is the meaning of work? Does my identity have to come from work? Will I, too, use work as an escape?

A question for you the reader: How might a man with this type of father respond to the women in his life? Think about it.

The *Macho Father* oozes strength and stability. He radiates perfection and has it all together. He doesn't need help and is very self-reliant. An excellent overseer, he wants others to notice his strength and masculinity. A son is his extension and must be masculine and successful, too. The son is pushed and any failure or mistake is unforgiven. If affection comes, it is given in a "masculine" manner and only if it has been earned. Stereotypes about male behavior are reinforced in this household.

This father also leaves quite a legacy: A strong model of responsibility and maleness—but the son wonders, *How do I live up to all this?* He has been given a distorted picture of what it means to be a man and his struggle will be to live up to it or challenge it.

What is lacking? The deficits in this relationship are seen and felt for years and they are many: A son may end up seeking to be like Dad with the same excessive macho image. He may rebel and throw away everything that Dad represented. He may choose to be a failure so he doesn't have to compete with his father. He may overemphasize his achievements. He needs to have his life under control to appear strong. Unable to express emotions, he may rely upon others to do so.

A question for you the reader: How might a man with this type of father respond to the women in his life? Think about it.

The Loving Father

There is one last type of father whom a few men experience. This is the *Loving, Accepting Father.* Choosing to be a father, he sacrificed other aspects of his life to fulfill this role. Both physically and emotionally present with his children, he chose to know and understand his son—and allowed his son to know and understand him as well. He could see life from other people's perspective. He invested time and himself in his family. He helped his son internalize his own values and become responsible. Since no one is perfect, there were disagreements and differences but these were resolved.

I believe every type of father described above carries the potential to become like this father. When a man allows Jesus Christ to invade and refine his life he can move toward a model of manhood which is balanced and complete, even with deficits in upbringing and family life. It is a man like this who leaves a rich legacy for a son.

The types of fathers we have just discussed are based on hundreds of interviews with men. Many fathers fit, to some degree, into one of these categories. We are not trying to pigeonhole people nor lay the blame at the feet of our fathers. Rather, we are trying to understand what may have occurred. This insight can help a man determine the type of man and father he would like to become.

This study of father-son relationships has led me to ask some different and significant questions in my premarital counseling with couples: "What did you receive from your father and what was lacking? If you become a father, what will you be able to give to your child(ren) and what may be lacking? What can you do now about what may be lacking?"

A son can receive what we all would like to have: love, warmth, unconditional acceptance, encouragement, being believed in, support and strength. There are other men in our lives besides our fathers who can give us these things. When we focus on the Word of God and its teachings and the model of Jesus Christ, the empty spaces can be filled.

To help a man understand his father and what it was like for him growing up, encourage your man to go to the nearest main branch of the public library and read a newspaper or news magazine for the week his father was born. Read all parts of the paper from local and world events to the advertisements. Encourage him to imagine what it was like to be both a child and a man at that time.

The four most desired gifts a son would like to receive from his father are: understanding, affection, approval and acceptance. How does the man in your life feel about his father? Whether it be your husband, close friend, son or even your own father, ask him these questions:

In what way did your father understand you?

In what way would you have liked or would like your father to understand you?

In what way did your father express affection to you?

In what way would you have liked or not liked him to express affection to you?

In what way did your father show you his approval of you?

In what would you have liked or not liked him to express his approval of you?

In what way did your father show that he accepted you?

In what way would you have liked your father or would like him now to demonstrate his acceptance of you?

What did your father teach you about what it means to be a man?

5

Men and Their Friends

The four of us—Tom, Jim, Steve, and I—had been hunting buddies for ages. Every chance we got, we would go out for deer, ducks, birds; whatever the season, we hunted it, and almost always together. We had some great times together, the four of us, despite the difference in our ages. It didn't matter because we really hit it off well. I think each of us thought of the other three as our best friends. We often said how we felt—we could talk about anything we wanted to in the group. Even the wives got to know each other pretty well. Once or twice a year we'd get together as couples. But mainly it was just a good group of guys all the way around.

I remember it was a Friday and we were all going to take off work at noon so we could drive out, set up camp, and be ready to go first thing in the morning. I had one of those four-wheel-drive trucks, so the plan was that I would pick everyone up. Steve lived farthest out, so we always picked him up last. As it turned out, I didn't get away from work as early as I hoped, and by the time I got Tom and Jim, we were running about an hour late. We pulled up in front of Steve's place and honked a couple of times. Usually he would have come running out, yelling and swearing about us being (late), but this time there was no sign of him. I saw his gear back by the garage, and I thought maybe he didn't hear us. Tom and Jim stayed in the truck while I went around to get him. He was in the backyard and he was dead. He had taken his shotgun, put the muzzle in his mouth, and with a piece of wood pushed the trigger and blown the back of his head away. He left a note near his body: "I'm sorry. There is no one to talk to."

At first I was just terribly angry. I was really angry at Steve. This was not some teenaged kid crazed out of his mind on drugs, or some guy down on his luck. He was thirty-one when he killed himself. He had a good job and a super wife. They weren't rich, but they didn't have any big debts or anything. I just couldn't see that he had any reason for doing what he did. It seemed so selfish. I remember thinking, "How could he do this to me? How could he say there was no one to talk to, when there was me?" I felt like I could have helped him, no matter what it was. We could talk about anything. At least I thought we could. Only later did it hit me that I didn't really know if we could talk about anything or not, because we never really talked about much that was personal.[1]

Men and their friendships. What are they really like? Do men tend to stand alone in isolation or are there great friendships which bind men together through thick and thin? Do women have a monopoly on meaningful, intimate friendships—or is this resource shared by both sexes?

What do you know about the friendships of the significant men in your life? Before you read on, I would like you to answer a few questions. If at all possible have the men in your life answer them as well. Using your answers and theirs, compare your discoveries with the remainder of the chapter. You might be surprised!

How many friends does this man have? (Remember to answer this before you ask the man for his response.)

Why does he consider them his friends?

What is the friendship based upon? What do they have in common?

If they didn't have those things in common, would there still be a friendship?

What would he miss if that friendship ended? How would he feel?

What does he talk about with his friends?

What feelings does he share with his friends?

Do these friends, or at least one of them, know him intimately? Does he share his joys, hurts, frustrations, concerns?

Does he depend or rely upon these friendships in any way?

Who were his friends as he was growing up? Does he still have them as friends?

Do his friendships change from time to time?

Now ask him to answer the above questions.

Think about these same questions as they apply to your own father whether he is alive or deceased. If he is still living, ask him these questions the next time you talk with him. If you have a son(s) ask him these questions after you have given your own responses.

Let's go back to the example of the four friends at the beginning of this chapter. The man who described his experience went on to say that what he and the others described as friendship was probably more of a casual and comfortable kind of "acquaintanceship." They talked about certain topics, but really did not share themselves.

Fact or Fiction?

All societies perpetuate certain myths which continue unchallenged. One of ours revolves around men and their friendships. Whether it be in song, story or myth, the friendships of men have been celebrated throughout history as the most unselfish of human relationships. Being a comrade in war, handling crisis together at work or playing side by side on the same athletic team, these relationships are described as the arenas for lifelong friendships. We have the image of friendships portrayed in films with Paul Newman and Robert Redford as Butch Cassidy and the Sundance Kid—two close friends bonded together against all odds.

Male friendships are portrayed as reflecting devotion, trust, honesty and selflessness with a high degree of loyalty. How much is fact and how much is fiction? Oh, it's true that men prefer the company of other men, but being with and opening up to other men are two different entities. Most men are really a bit wary of other men and many of their relationships are shallow, superficial and limited as to the depth that can ever occur. For most men, adolescence is the last time they remember having intense same-sex relationships.[2]

Many years ago land in the West had no fences or barriers. As far as the eye could see, there were miles and miles of unbroken plains and gentle slopes. If you were to ride through that land you would not encounter barriers which would hinder your wandering. There would have been freedom.

Today it is difficult to find open land. Fences, barriers and even signs are ever present telling you "Keep out! No trespassing!"

There are similar barriers to friendships. When men and women enter a room they begin sizing each other up. The men respond to the women by giving them compliments. They are quick to notice what they admire and like. Why? Because most men have given considerable thought to what they like in women. They know what pleases them.

It is just the opposite with their own sex. Most men are not able to define what they like or do not like in other men. We just haven't given it that much thought. Men are more hesitant to give compliments to another man or tell the man how much they value his personal qualities.

The Walls Between

Men play it safe and erect walls between themselves and other men. Dr. Ken Druck has identified several of the most common barriers or walls which men use to hide behind. Each is its own variation of a "no trespassing" sign.

There is *the wall of competition.* Two men meet for the first time and introduce themselves. What is each thinking? Let's open up their minds and take a look. Often their thoughts are quite simple. "How much better a man am I than he? How much less a man am I than he?" Those who use the wall of competition are constantly comparing themselves to other men. This wall contains bricks labeled job, title, money and status symbols (such as the label on the suit the other man is wearing or whether he drives a BMW, Jaguar or Honda). These value comparisons of another person's worth keep a man from appreciating the real uniqueness and quality in the other person. The wall of competition is a reflection of low self-esteem. To overcome this, comparisons are used to establish self-worth.

A second barrier is *the wall of women.* There are men who use the women in their lives to act as a buffer between themselves and other men. This could include a wife, girlfriend, mother or even a secretary. It is a convenient way of avoiding contact with other men. Why do they do this? Because of shyness or lack of social skills. Women are used as peacemakers, go-betweens, mediators—especially when a man feels discomfort with other men, whether it be in social situations or the work place. A woman can keep the conversation going. But most men would have difficulty admitting they use women in this way. They would explain it in other ways.

The wall of fear is quite common. None of us enjoys rejection, judgment or criticism by other men. Whether we admit it or not, we are sensitive to what other men think of us. These insecurities are kept hidden because if other people knew they might use it against us.

Men live with a sense of discomfort in their man-to-man relationships. The fear of relating and sharing their deepest feelings covers many issues. They live with the fear of being intimate and yet experience isolation and loneliness when they are not. Few are comfortable in sharing their down times, including worries, disappointments or failures, for fear of being rated as weak and unmasculine. In one way or another, men measure each other. They are also reluctant to share their successes or times of delight over an achievement because of the fear of appearing boastful or, worse, inciting competitive jealousies.

In Joel Block's in-depth survey of over 500 men, he found 84 percent would not fully disclose themselves to other men, and only 8 of 100 said they have ever had a frank sexual discussion with a male friend.[3] Men are hesitant and anticipate an attack. How tragic! How healthy and freeing it is when we can lower the barricades and invite another person to become a part of our lives.

If a man is given a choice of confidants with whom to share fears, concerns and doubts, he is twice as likely to talk to a woman as to a man. Half of the men in this study confided in no one![4] Some men prefer sharing with strangers. I experience this in my counseling or at seminars out of state when men approach me to share. Bartenders hear more secrets than most of us counselors do. Strangers pour their hearts out to them.

What About Touching?

Men also fear that if they get too close to other men and share their feelings they might be suspected of being gay. Touching is all right on the playing field or when celebrating something extraordinary. Close male friends in other countries such as the Mediterranean area often show their friendship by warm hugs, touching one another and slapping one another on the back.[5] But seldom does this happen in the Western world.

When I first encountered some men in churches who greeted me with a hug or held my hand longer than usual, it was an adjustment. I wasn't used to it. But I quickly adjusted. Hugging and touching is a vital and healthy form of expression. Men can relearn and overcome their hesitation.[6]

A man does not openly express affection with other men because he fears being considered unmasculine. Even with a very close relationship, the verbal expression of affection does not come easily. A man will do something for a friend, give flattery through an insult or even share with another person or a group how he feels about the man, rather than expressing his feeling directly to his friend.

A man who co-taught a class of high school boys shared his experience. "I knew that my friend Tom liked me. We've been doing things together for years. I really found out how much he liked me in our class the other day. The kids were asking questions about what love really is. Tom was encouraging them to come up with ideas and images of different types of love. He gave examples of how he loved his mother, his wife, his son and then he pointed at me and said, 'And I love Frank, too.' It really made me feel great. We've never talked about it, but we do love each other."

If a man is going to develop intimacy with another man, he will have to be willing to counter the standard of society which dictates what it means to be a man and a friend to another man. He will need to overcome his own fears about disclosing himself and be willing to handle some of the rejection he will undoubtedly meet. By doing this, however, he may threaten other men who are not yet at the place of being willing to risk.

Types of Friendships

Some men have close friends. Most have a number of acquaintances. Let's look at several types of friendships men have with other men. Remember, however, that friendships progress over time and a friend can be moved from one category to another.

Have you ever wondered why men enjoy some of the *groups* they are in? You may have thought, *What does he see in that bunch of guys? Why does he like to spend so much time with them? It seems like such a waste. I ask him why and he says "I enjoy them." How can you enjoy someone if you don't talk that much?*

There are many reasons why a man is drawn to other men—similarity in lifestyle, the way they wear their clothes, enjoy the same sports, drink or the way they talk or don't talk. A man may imitate another, try to learn from him or help him. Some relationships are developed to learn from the person such as the mentor.

Identification with a certain group will fill some of his needs. He may enjoy the group's acceptance of him. He may learn to value himself as an equal. The comradeship a man feels with others gives him a feeling of self-affirmation. Team sports give a man the opportunity to identify with the group but at the same time still feel like an individual. Belonging to a group can affirm old values. The belongingness assures familiarity and a place where a man can relax with others who feel the same way. Men do like to be close to other men, but it is safer within the group context. Sometimes a man is hesitant to go out with just one other couple, but feels more comfort in a group of new couples.

Some men do have a *Best Friend.* This is a man who will stick with me during the best and the worst of times, a person I know as intimately as possible. I have no fear of sharing my inner struggles, thoughts or feelings with him. I can trust him implicitly. Both of us can take the risk of expressing our displeasure or anger, our concern and affection for one another and generally open up on any subject. This type of friendship is developed over a period of time, entails a willingness to take risks and even survives major disagreements. I have seen many Christian men who are able to have this relationship because Jesus Christ's presence has overcome the fears and barriers. I have experienced this type of friendship. We talk, laugh and cry together—and when the relationship isn't there, we feel the emptiness.

The *Good Buddy* is the type of friend you can call on in the time of need. He is available when needed but this friendship has limitations on closeness. These men actually care about other men more than they admit. But the care and affection are expressed through being available and reliable rather than open sharing. Or hitting one another on the arm saying, "How ya doing, you old _____ ." There is a line drawn. A wife, knowing how her husband feels about this good buddy, may ask, "Why don't you ever talk about how you feel about one another? Just tell him." The husband may reply with, "There's no need to—we know."

The *Party Friend* is available when a man wants the company of another man for a good time. This could be fishing, playing ball, hunting or going to a sporting event. Conversation is superficial and deals with topics which arise at the time. Feelings and concerns are not usually discussed. These friendships share good times but they are not used for support or consolation when one of them has a need.

Competition can be a basis for such a friendship. Mutual liking and respect can draw two men together, but the desire to compete keeps the relationship on a fragile level. They see one another as equals. In fact, the reflection of themselves which they saw in each other confirmed their friendship.

When the good time is over, each man knows the friendship will be there for the next occasion. Little thought will be given to the other person until the next event.

The *Friend from the Past* is the one with a common history. We went to school together years ago or played on the same team. Perhaps we lived next door to each other. These friendships are enjoyable because they bring back a raft of memories and we delight in the time of reminiscing. When two such friends get together, they seem to enter a time warp and slip back into the past with their stories and jokes and even sometimes the way they act. They don't usually have much involvement with each others' present life unless they decide it would be enjoyable to rebuild the relationship. Recently I have discovered a couple of friends from my high school years who live near me. I am looking forward to spending more time with them to build a present relationship since we have much in common.

Many of us have *Institutional Friends.* These friendships come about and are maintained by association at work, church, service clubs and so on. Men in this setting connect on a set of guidelines and are quite predictable in how they relate. Belonging to something in common is the basis for the relationship and little is risked between the men. Most of them (unless closer relationships are desired and built) play it safe. When the common ground is no longer there, they rarely see each other again nor do they give much thought to one another.[6]

Then there is the *Mentor* relationship. This is a unique relationship for you to be aware of. It can be a bit complex, but is very important for a man in early adulthood. The mentor is usually a few years older who has more experience in the world the younger man is entering. This man is seen as *both* a peer and an adviser or teacher as well. The mentor is very important in helping the young man attain his dream. He can act as a teacher or guide. He can provide counsel and moral support during times of stress; he believes in the younger man and encourages him. These relationships between a mentor and a "mentee" last from two or three years to as long as eight years. They often end when one moves, changes jobs or even dies. Some end totally in a friendly fashion or with strong conflict and bad feelings. Some younger men break away since they want to be their "own person." Some develop into solid friendships when the mentor encourages the younger man to rise to his level of competence and is not threatened by sharing the equality. Both function as equals. This takes much time, discussion and openness—but it is possible.

Too many men today still maintain they don't *need* friends. That is why they don't have close personal relationships. Men say:

"I don't see what women find to spend so much time talking about. Maybe they need to talk that much and share that much, but not me. I can handle it myself."

"I don't have what you would call close friends. I don't belong to any groups as such. I go to church and to the classes, but I don't belong. I don't see any real need for any more involvement."

"I know a lot of guys and we can shoot the breeze. I like them, but don't need to get any closer. I don't want to spend any time with them."

"Friendships can be a pain in the neck at times. It takes

time and I don't know if I'd be any better off than I am now."

"If I need the friendship of another man, that means I can't make it on my own. I don't like that. If I relate to another guy, it's because I want to, not because I need to."

Men see time spent with other men as having a task-oriented purpose. A woman asks another woman to lunch and the one says, "Oh, great. I'd love to." A man asks another man to lunch and he says, "All right. What's up?" What do we have to accomplish? The relationship is not high on the list of objectives.

Friendship means something very different to men than it does to women. Even if there is a close intimate relationship between one man and another, it rarely approaches the depth of openness which occurs between women. The friendship of two women is real friendship. Few men reveal much of their personal and private selves to other men.

Many Friends?

The typical male friendship pattern is to have "many friends," each of whom knows something about the person but no one individual knows very much. No other man has all the information about him. If he has ten "friends," it would take all ten of them coming together and sharing the fragments of information they have about him to try and construct who this man is. Most friendships originate in the context of common occupational or recreational interests.

A man's friends can include a neighbor, a weekly racquetball partner, an acquaintance, a co-worker or someone he runs into each Wednesday at his business club meeting. And he relates differently to each one. He knows both the limits and the potential of each relationship. He might talk to his racquetball friend about how hard his job is, but he won't tell him about the run-in he had with his employer. He may share with his luncheon friend about the run-in, but not share his feelings of hurt over the situation. He may even share with a good friend that the problem led to his having to find a new job. But he probably won't share about his feelings, hurt, rejection and fear over finding a new job as soon as possible. He limits what he shares.

For men, friendships are often slow to develop and this increases their hesitation about establishing intimate relationships with others. A man's career, family and identity take up his time and energy during his twenties and thirties. It may take him until his forties to realize that he is lacking in male relationships. His former friendships have probably faded. A man finishes high school and goes to college. College friendships often die as each goes his own way. There is a danger in failing to cultivate these friendships. A man, whether he realizes it or not, may become overly dependent upon women in his life for companionship and caring. The loneliness weighs heavily upon older men as evidenced by the fact that single or widowed men in this category have a death rate twice that of women in a similar situation.

The lack of depth in his male relationships is often evident when things are going well since (unfortunately) most men prefer to be somewhat isolated during a crisis or a celebration. This is directly contrary to the guidelines of scripture where we are told to rejoice with those who rejoice and weep with those who weep. Men do not invite others to join them in their delight or despair.

What do men *talk about*? Whatever it is, it is talked *about* with very little revelation about one's personal self. Sports is high on the list of topics from childhood on through adulthood. From participation he moves into becoming a spectator who enjoys discussing his own past exploits and those of the teams he watches. Younger unmarried men discuss sex almost as much.

Gossip is as prevalent among men as it is with women. Men tend to talk about other men in terms of their performance, achievement and competence rather than their character. Other men are talked about in terms of what they do and what they don't do rather than who they are. Rarely are their qualities of character discussed.

Have you ever listened to male humor? Do you understand it or does it puzzle you? Male humor tends to be different from yours. Insults often are a main theme. Men love to take jibes at others, but it is usually limited to what is apparent to everyone else and not deeply personal.

A man's looks, whether it be his hairline or shape, his

performance, behavior or speech, are all subjects of humor. These insults have a light-hearted tone and are accepted in that way, returned in kind. Some of this humor is hard for women to understand and is an approach they would find difficult to use. It is learned early in childhood and increases as relationships evolve.

Three mornings a week I play racquetball and you would be fascinated at the conversations which occur in the locker room. There is factual interaction about work, very little about family, quite a bit about professional sports activities and a lot of good-natured exchanging of insults. I have an increasingly receding hairline which is a favorite target for many of the men I've interacted with for the past four years.

Our style of humor, however, can serve as a barrier to real intimacy. If a man tries to introduce some personal feelings and concerns into a group such as this, it will probably be rejected. The other men would be uncomfortable with it and would respond with kidding or making a joke of it. If what a man shares is rejected by others, the man can still save face by saying he was only joking.

There are some men who can share on the deepest levels without fearing the response of others. I have seen it and I have experienced it. Once the initial fear or embarrassment is overcome, the risk is more than rewarded by the results. Men who know Jesus Christ as their personal Lord have an entirely new world available to them. But it still takes time, effort and risk to overcome our societal conditioning.

There are many men who are envious of women's friendships. Unfortunately, it is usually when a man needs friendship the most that he discovers what is lacking in his own friendships. Hear the thoughts of several men: "We men get emotional hernias. We try to carry all the load ourselves when we have a problem. But women have learned to share their problems and in turn the load is less. Why can't I?"

"My wife got over the death of our child much sooner than I did. It still hangs on me. She talked about it so much with her friends. Maybe that's why she did. I just didn't feel it was anything I could talk over with anyone. I guess I still don't. I tried once with a friend, but it seemed like he didn't know how to handle it."

"I guess the difference is, women talk their way through things and men *think* their way through them. When you talk, you do it with somebody. But not with thinking. You do that alone. But you end up in the same place because you don't have another person's perspective to help you."[7]

Men are told they have to choose between manly strength and being expressive with others which can lead to deep relationships. Most men do not open up unless driven to the wall, to despair—and even then it is not easy. This reinforces the tendency men have to see sharing as weakness. Self-disclosure and expressiveness are associated with problems. This leads to shallow relationships between men.

In your interactions with men, you may find yourself encouraging a man to develop some deep friendships. He may give you a number of reasons why he doesn't or won't. Or he may ask, "What's in it for me?" If so, here are some reasons you can give him.

The Value of Close Friendships

Ken Druck has identified some of the benefits for men who develop deep male friendships. Once a man opens himself up to another man who is also willing, each learns that he is not alone in his fears, insecurities and desires. There have been times when I have had inner "wonderings" about myself and through the honest sharing with another man face to face (or even through reading the inner thoughts of a man in a book), I discovered that nothing was wrong with me. I was normal!

By developing close friendships, men can lessen their dependencies on women. In a sense, men have been taught that only women can help them satisfy their emotional needs and thus men are not even considered for that purpose. This can often lead to a dependency on women which becomes emotionally out of balance. By developing friendships with other men, a man's emotional balance can be restored and his marriage strengthened since there will be less emotional dependency. But don't be surprised if this idea is rejected by a man when you share it with him! Few men want to admit to emotional neediness.

A man who shares himself intimately will develop greater self-confidence and self-esteem. His willingness to share reflects a solid self-esteem. He is freer to trust others.

Male friends help one another in times of difficulty and crisis over the women in their lives. The sharing, insight and help are essential. I find myself in a unique position since I am a marriage counselor. I listen to the inner concerns, fears, frustrations and hurts of many men. I work with them and their marital relationships. I share as a counselor, but I also share as a man. They learn from me and I often learn from them. Our interaction frequently focuses on their distorted beliefs about the role of a man. What a delight it is to see men open up and share their feelings with the women in their lives—and the men! I find this type of ministry helping me to continue to share and be open with others. It is easy to retreat and move back into an emotional cavern.

A male friend helps us handle life's stresses and crises. The survivors are those who do not attempt to handle the problems of life all by themselves. They have a friend who walks with them and is willing to be a buffer. I guess the older I grow, the more direct I become in my discussions with men. I was encouraging a man to begin to reach out and develop some male relationships and he asked, "What's in it for me? How will it help?"

I looked at him and said simply, "If you want to live longer and stay healthy, get a friend. If you want to get sick and die too soon, stay the way you are. It's your choice." I did get the reaction I wanted from him. Sometimes shock techniques are the only way!

Whether a man admits it or not, loneliness hurts. God did not create us to live in isolation and to be alone. Friends help to lift the loneliness of life and balance our needs.

Friendships provide us with some excellent resources when we need them. Other men can give us support, information, advice, companionship and professional networking. It is far better to live with a spirit of cooperation than competition.[8]

Is there any future for men and deep intimate friendships? Yes! More and more men are discovering the potential. As men have begun to share child care, become more involved at home and redefine their roles at an earlier age, they are discovering the need and delight of friendships. Sensitivity can be a benefit. As the myth of what it means to be a male begins to break down, men are saying, "I want deep friendships and relationships—with my wife and with other men." It is a slow process and we see more of the change with men in their mid-thirties and forties. The task now is to assist young men in this process and present new models to our children.

Talk with men about their friendships. Raise the possibilities of new types of friendships. Encourage them to give it a try. After all, if they have tried life without friends, they know what that is like. What have they got to lose by trying life with friends? You may want to encourage your man or your church to develop men's study groups and to read *The Friendless American Male* by David Smith (Regal Books) and *The Secrets Men Keep* by Ken Druck (Doubleday).

6

Feelings—The Great Male Struggle

He sat there with his head in his hands looking at the floor. "John," his wife asked, "are you okay?"

"Sure, just thinking," came the reply.

"It looks like something is bothering you. You seem kind of worried this evening."

"Oh, no. It's nothing."

"But it seems like there is. You don't usually sit around holding your head in your hands. Maybe it would help if you could talk about it."

"Nothing to talk about. Now, quit prying."

"I'm not prying. I'm concerned. You're just not yourself tonight."

"If you're concerned, quit prying. It's all right, I tell you."

"But I just want you to talk to me and let me know what's bothering you."

"I am talking. The only thing bothering me is you're pestering me to tell you what's wrong. What's wrong is you're not leaving me alone!"

Conversations like these are common. All the signs are there that something is bothering this man. But once again the great male hesitation arises—the fear or inability to share deep inner feelings.

Men tend to be like the medieval castles of old. They erect high walls and water-filled moats to protect themselves. Limiting their emotional expression gives them a sense of being in control. They decide who can enter their lives and when that person can do so. The drawbridge remains closed and the man feels safe and secure from attack. But staying behind the walls too long makes the man a prisoner of his own making and he slowly begins to die.

Where Is Your Castle?

Every person needs love. But the castle-dweller soon becomes a prisoner without love, as one by one people give up attempting to penetrate the fortress. Erected walls have a way of growing higher and higher until we can no longer look over them to see who it is we might be keeping out.

I have actually heard women say, "I live with a portable fortress. He walks around the house with walls on all sides and a 'keep out' sign hung around his neck. I've tried blasting through the walls, digging a tunnel underneath with dynamite, pole-vaulting over the walls and nothing works. He's won . . . but I don't think he knows the cost of his victory."

The walls you see men carrying about are defenses. They're there to protect and help him keep his distance. These walls hide hurts, insecurities, frustrations, joys, sorrows and even love. To build walls men use bricks of laughter, silence, intellectualization and withdrawal.

Men *are* more silent than women about their feelings. But that's not all! Many do not even notice that feelings are there! And a lot of them like it that way. One man told me, "I've got better things to do than take my emotional temperature all the time." In a counseling session a wife asked her husband, "Honey, how do you feel about that?"

He turned to her and said, factually and simply, "I don't feel anything about it. I'm a simple person. I'm not afraid, nor sad, nor do I have any regrets. I don't tell you about my feelings because they aren't there. Can you get that through your head?" It is quite likely that this man's feelings were so deeply buried he had shut himself off from his conscious mind.

Macho Man?

The real man depicted for us is most often found in movies portrayed by actors like John Wayne or Sylvester Stallone. On TV you can take your choice over the past two decades from

Magnum P.I. to *Police Story.* Real men do show the emotions of rage, anger, vengeance, envy, lust and greed, but sensitivity, tenderness and personal caring for another man are quite lacking. Recently I saw the movie *Top Gun,* the story of the Navy's top fighter pilots. The male macho image presented was well illustrated in the main character, "Maverick," who could not fully grieve or cry for his closest friend when he died. The "Be strong and keep your chin up" male image had to be protected.

Even though the once top-rated TV show *Miami Vice* has the classical police and villain format, vulnerability and sensitivity are emerging in a strange new way, making it an unusual and unique show. In a recent article in the *Los Angeles Times,* a detailed analysis of this show gave extensive food for thought. The three leading male characters show a sensitivity which is often absent in other portrayals. They are vulnerable men who are learning to relate to others and exhibit individual compassion for each other. These men are aware that their efforts to handle drug dealers and other manifestations of vice will have minimal results. There is a sadness about the stories since often more questions are raised than answered. But human emotions do come across even though they are minimally shared with words.

Men have a need to preserve their masculine image which unfortunately prevents them from being transparent with other men. To preserve this image they must not reveal their vulnerability or weaknesses because they fear the other person's response and they do not want to appear effeminate. The most graphic description of men and their emotions comes from a book, *The Hazards of Being Male:*

> The male has become anesthetized and robotized because he has been heavily socialized to repress and deny almost the total range of his emotions and human needs in order that he can perform in the acceptable "masculine" way. Feelings become unknown, unpredictable quantities, the expression of which threaten him and make him feel vulnerable. By the time he is a mature adult, he also has undoubtedly surrounded himself with a family environment that has a heavy stake in his continuing non-feeling and in subtle ways reinforces his functioning as a well oiled machine.[1]

Men today are urged to "get in touch with their feelings." And they ask, "Why? What will it do for me? You want me to give up my way of living, my defense structure? What are you offering me?" Other men who indicate a willingness to do this say, "How? I just don't know how to do what you're asking."

The Masks Men Wear

Men have learned various means of resisting the expression of their feelings. They do this to let others know that emotional expression and survival in this world do not mix.

Some men are *cynical*. For them all feelings are phony. They view themselves and other's expressions with bitterness and a resignation. "Your feelings and even mine are insincere, so why bother?"

Some men are so *independent* they consider feelings only an expression of weakness. Feelings indicate you need someone else, but if you open yourself up you will be taken advantage of by the other guy.

I'm sure you're aware of the man who uses his *intellect* to defend against emotional expression. He dissects and analyzes and will discuss feelings but nothing personal comes out of him. His responses are flat and devoid of any personal expression. He uses his intellect as a filter to cleanse his expressions of any hint of emotion.

Some men express their defenses through *passive-aggressiveness*. They say, "Gee! I don't know what you want. What do you want me to feel?" Nonengagement is their way of defending against feelings. They make others try to draw their feelings from them and in time they give up since it doesn't work.

The *manipulative* man hurts people and leaves feelings of betrayal in his wake. He uses people and drops them when he is finished with them. He mimics any feeling which he senses they want, since this will help him get what he desires. His goals are achieved by fooling others with a flash expression of feelings.

You will meet some men who will tell you, "Look, I can express any emotion and feeling I so desire when I want to, but most of the time it is a waste of time. What does it get you? I have too much to accomplish to let feelings get in the way. They will just hold me back." The man who says this is fooling himself since he really doesn't know how to express those feelings.[2]

The dilemma which men experience and feel is best described by Ken Olson as he talks about the loneliness of a man:

> There it is again!
> A twinge of pain?
> Forget it. It will go away.
> In the business of my day.
> I've places to go and things to do . . .
> A round of meetings with entrepreneurs.
> Planes to catch and taxis to hail,
> I have life by the tail.
> But what is this painful wail?
> From the depths of me I ache.
> It greets me when I wake.
> Even in a crowded room of people
> I can hear a haunting toll from a church bell steeple.
> There's nothing wrong with me.
> I'm a success, as anyone can see.
> I—I hurt. I feel an emptiness.
> This feeling, is it loneliness?
> Loneliness?
> I'm married with children, three.
> Yet at times I feel so alone.
> Maybe it's time to come down from my throne.
> It's not good for a man to be alone.[3]

Men use clever techniques to bottle up their feelings. In addition to the ones already expressed I have heard other responses such as, "These feelings will go away. No big deal." And little importance is given to them.

Believe it or not, men do worry, but they keep that to themselves and they are often anxious about what they are feeling. Worry is one of their defenses. Keeping busy makes feelings disappear. (Or does it?)

Many of us men confuse women by changing our feelings into other sentiments. For example, men are quite adept at expressing anger. And often the recipient is sidetracked by this smokescreen and is led away from the real feeling. I see anger as a symptom. Underlying most anger are three other feelings:

hurt, fear or frustration. It is difficult for some to come out and share the fact, "I am really frightened. I am scared that this proposal is not right and then our company will be in difficulty. And I feel responsible for it."

Frustration is usually caused by unmet needs and expectations—and often these are also unexpressed as well. The lack of expression is what creates the frustration. I have talked with angry men and on several occasions I have purposely ignored their angry tirades and looked at them and softly stated, "I hear your anger but I'm wondering what you are really feeling. Could it be that you are experiencing hurt at this time? Is there something that you are afraid of? Could there be a frustration that you are dealing with right now? I'd like to hear what it might be." And often I have been surprised by the acceptance of the invitation to share their true feeling. They realize as I do that their anger is a smokescreen and a form of denial of the real feeling.

Men hide behind their roles to escape feelings: "I don't have to share my feelings with you because I'm the head of the house and what I say is the way it's going to be around here."

Filing Our Feelings

Some men store their feelings in an inner file just hoping that the file drawer is closed forever. Others use their wives as a defense against their own feelings. How? Carefully and subtly. They encourage emotional expression on the part of their wives so that they do not have to hear them say, "But we do not share feelings in our relationship!"

Avoidance is often used by threatened men. Situations, events and even people are avoided. I know of some men who are very uncomfortable visiting the home where our retarded son Matthew lives. It's not always comfortable for me either, but those feelings have meaning and purpose. And they can be handled. Men are sometimes terrified by the feeling that they may be losing control and may cry uncontrollably because of the extensive mental and physical retardation they see when they walk onto Matthew's ward.

Just recently I experienced a worship service at our church which was hard to handle for many, men and women alike. Once a year we have an emphasis upon the handicapped. And many handicapped individuals take part in this service. The scripture is read by a blind person reading from the braille Bible. Each time we have been in this service, a beautiful young woman with MS instructs us in singing "Spirit of the Living God" in sign language. We sing it with both words and sign at first and then as the organ plays, the entire congregation signs it silently with their hands. We hear testimonies of how the presence of God has made such a difference in the life of a quadriplegic, a deaf person, a blind pianist and others.

This service is one I would not miss, and at the same time part of me wants to get up and leave because of the intensity of my emotional response. I am afraid that I will break down and weep uncontrollably because of joy; experiencing the blessings, recalling the hurting experience with our son and seeing individuals visibly handicapped make me wish I could reach out and heal but I cannot. I guess there is a bit of frustration there and once again the question of "O God, why?" arises from the depths. But I wouldn't miss this service, for it is a reminder of the grace of God and the meaning that he gives to life. As I sat there recently I thought, *This service really is for all of us, for we are all handicapped. The difference is, we can see their handicaps and ours are not so visible. We are all people in need of the strengthening hand of Jesus Christ.* In time, some of our handicaps will come to the surface and become more apparent.

Healing Our Emotions

But the great male handicap can be healed. Our stunted emotional growth does not have to be permanent. Often we need a woman to help us on that journey.

Men often ask the question, "Why should I share my feelings? What's in it for me?" If a man can come to the place where he views his feelings as a friend and not an enemy, he will discover the various benefits.

Feelings are a tremendous source of energy. They're like an electrical socket which motivates and challenges us to move ahead.

Feelings create a healthy environment for the man and those around him. Sharing his feelings clears the air and allows for growth and resolution of differences. Ventilating feelings is one of the best stress-reducers for both men and women.

Feelings are the bridge which connect a man to another individual. Relating to another person with feelings creates a closer bond than do mere thoughts. Sharing feelings enables a person to trust others.

Feelings enable us to make wise and proper decisions. Believe it or not, those who are in touch with their feelings are often in a better position to make difficult decisions and take proper action than those who are not. The intuitive side of a person is a necessary complement to the factual. Intuition often gives us the confirmation we are looking for when making a key decision.

Feelings help us to understand hurts from the past and enable us to allow those old wounds to heal. Forgiveness is possible both intellectually and emotionally. There are times that we need to rely upon our intellect when feelings are lacking, but in time the use of the one helps the other come alive.

Feelings are a source of growth for a person. We learn much about ourselves by experiencing, identifying and sharing a feeling in an atmosphere of trust and safety.[4]

One of the important reasons for this emphasis upon feeling ties into intimacy. There can be no real intimacy in a relationship without the expression of feelings. Intimacy involves a special relationship, an emotional closeness, and involves understanding and being understood by another significant person. Intimacy also involves a bond of affection based upon mutual caring, responsibility, trust, open communication of feelings and sensations as well as sharing significant emotional responses.

Emotional expression is evident in love. When a person voluntarily discloses himself and his revelations and feelings about himself to us, we feel loved. This disclosure is so important in love and intimacy because it conveys the giving of oneself to another. It is all right to ask yourself, "How much has this man told me about himself?" Consider the men in your life. What do you really know about their inner beliefs, values and feelings? Ask and keep asking but vary your approach.

Every person has a public and a private side. The public side is open to most people but the private side is guarded and available to a select few or none at all! How do you discover a man's private side when there is little expression?

Some women say that the way they discover more about their husband's private side is by what he dislikes, discards and rejects. Here are some actual statements from wives:

"He doesn't tell me what he likes but I always know what he doesn't like. He feels free to share that at least."

"I sometimes wonder if it isn't a game with him. I feel he gets some enjoyment out of making me guess what he likes and doesn't like."

"What bothers me is, he will tell me that it doesn't matter what we have for dinner or where we go out for dinner. But then he gripes about what I serve or where we go. It's just hard to figure him out."

"I learned about my husband's style of dress from what he chose out of the closet. He likes me to buy his clothes, so I do. The ones he never chooses I send to my brother since they're like new. It works out pretty well for us. And now I am able to choose those items which he likes. In his way he has told me. Yet . . ."

One of the many challenges a wife experiences is to get her husband to be specific in his preferences. When you have to guess all the time what a man likes and dislikes, you end up feeling unloved. Why? A loving relationship is built upon two people revealing themselves to one another.

Men and women both talk about their work and money but in different ways. Women openly discuss both work and money, but men tend to say much more through their behavior. Often a woman has to dig and assume about her spouse's work and many concerns since firsthand information is not always available. Men do not tend to give a blow-by-blow description of what occurred at work. Interpersonal information is usually lacking as men tend to focus upon tasks rather than people relationships.

One way to learn about these areas is to notice the behavioral clues which your man gives. When concerned about work or finances, some men come home from the office and immediately go out to work in the yard. Some don't eat. In time you can learn what these behaviors mean. Some men yell at the dog, some drink, some are quieter than usual and some may be irritable. What can you do? Express an invitation to share what happened at work or what is occurring with the finances.

Wives tell me they make observations as an invitation to share. Their statements include, "I noticed you're not eating tonight. Anything going on at work?" "I sense you're a bit upset. Is something bothering you?" "You're quieter than usual. I'm willing to hear what's going on in your mind. You probably don't want me to play twenty questions with you to find out. Like to tell me?"

Do men automatically respond in a positive, open manner to these invitations? In time, some do. The typical response is defensiveness as the man denies that anything is wrong. If he does admit that something is amiss, he is still defensive in that he will swear and pledge that his situation is temporary, within his control, of no real importance and really not worth discussing. Would you like to hear the typical comments? In fact, some wives say they can predict in advance their husband's statements because they are so predictable.

"Oh, there's a little problem but nothing that I can't handle."

"It's not worth taking the time to talk about it. It'll pass."

"Why talk? What can you do about the problems at work?"

"I'll pass. Besides, I'm praying about it and that's enough."

"I didn't want to worry you with this. You have enough on your mind."

"I'll work it out in time. What's for dinner?"

At times it appears that men want their work and money matters to remain a mystery.

Up Close and Personal

Not only do men have a private side, but they have a personal side which is even more private! Women can learn about men's private sides through their preferences, choices and the opinions they express. But learning how a man thinks and feels about himself is totally dependent upon the man's willingness to share.

What do you know about the first man in your life? How did your father feel about himself and how did he deal with those feelings? How much did he share with you? How much do you know about your husband or that special man in your life? What do you ask and how do you go about it?

It's not surprising that men are such reluctant revealers of information about their deepest personal feelings since other less personal information is often not shared either. This lack of sharing is one of the critical reasons for distance occurring between a husband and wife. And the problem is brought into focus often when the children leave the home and both the husband and wife are faced with the lack of closeness. Often the man does not feel the need for sharing and disclosure.

Even during times of crisis that involve personal losses, emotional responses vary. Men tend to avoid the disclosure of their personal responses which often leads others to feel they don't care as much or they are trying to deal with their feelings by themselves. No matter what the reason, this leads to the wife feeling shut out and isolated. The husband's stoicism is seen as indifference.[5]

Men have been asked why they don't share their feelings with their wives. In survey after survey, the responses are similar. Many are defensive.

"She knows—or should know—how I feel. I really don't need to tell her."

"I don't really feel the need to talk about this."

"That's just the way I am. And that's just the way most men are. Women are different and they're just going to have to get used to that fact. So I don't reveal a lot of the stuff inside of me. That doesn't mean I don't love her. It's just me."

"I didn't realize you were interested, that you wanted to know about it."

"I thought I told you!"

"I really want to tell you, but I just can't find the right time to share this."

"I'm not certain how you're going to handle what I say. And I don't want you getting upset or having to talk about this for the next hour. It's easier to keep quiet."

"Look, you just wouldn't understand. And that leads to more and more questions and I get tired of talking about work. I want to leave it there."

"I'll tell you what would help me share more with my wife. For me to open up with her, there has to be no risk. I can be honest but I don't want to be hassled. I don't want to be judged for what I share and I want to share for as long as I want—and then have the freedom to quit when I need to."

What did you hear from these men? What were their concerns and fears about sharing?

Michael McGill describes this situation well when he says, ". . . Most wives live with and love men who are in some very fundamental ways strangers to them—men who withhold themselves and, in doing so, withhold their love. These wives may be loved, but they do not feel loved because they do not know their husbands. They do not know love."[6]

The Women Speak

"Men think too much. There's more to life than thinking," she said as she sat in the group of women discussing the question, "How do men's emotional responses differ from women's?" The others nodded in agreement. Several of the other thirty- to forty-year-old women shared their observations and feelings which turned out to be very accurate.

"I wish he didn't think he always had to define everything. I feel as if I've been talking to a dictionary. Every week for the past year my husband has said, 'What do you mean? I can't talk to you if I don't understand your words. Give me some facts, not those darn feelings!' Well, sometimes I can't give him facts and definitions. Man shall not live by definitions alone!"

Another woman spoke up and said, "I don't think that men understand the difference between sharing their feelings and what they *think* about their feelings. They tend to intellectualize so much of the time. Why do men have to think about how they feel? Just come out with it unedited. He doesn't have to respond like a textbook or edit everything he shares. I wonder if the emotional side of a man threatens him? Of course you can't always control your emotional responses. So what?"

A woman sitting across from her added her perspective to the discussion. "My husband is an engineer and you ought to be around when his engineer friends come over. The house is like a cerebral, cognitive conference! All logical facts. They walk in with their slide rules and calculators, and it's as though the house were swept clean of any emotional response. They talk but don't disclose. They share, but on the surface. They're safe and secure. Sometimes I have this urge to come into the room and start sharing emotions with all sorts of emotional words and then start crying and see how long it would take for some of them to bolt out the door, jump out the window or hide their face behind a magazine. Why, I could threaten ten men inside of a minute. I never realized what power I had. I think I'll do that next time they're over." It took a while for the laughter to subside among the group.

The Men Reply

I would concur with these women's observations. I have seen hundreds of men like this in the counseling office and in marriage seminars throughout the country over the past twenty years. But what do men say about this? Listen to four men's comments.

"I understand her need to talk about us and our relationship. I happen to think that there is a right and a wrong way to talk about those things. If you're not careful, the whole thing can get out of hand. It's best to be as rational as possible. If you let it get too emotional, you never can make any good decisions, and if it gets too personal, someone could get hurt. A little bit of distance goes a long way where a lot of these things are concerned."

"It's important first to set out clearly what the issues are. I don't think that women do this very well. They latch on to the first thing that comes to mind, get totally emotionally involved in it. The next thing you know, you're arguing about everything under the sun, and no one is happy. I believe in a clear definition of the problem at the outset. If she can tell me exactly what is bothering her, we can deal with it logically. If she can't do that, then there is no sense even talking about it."

94 □ H. Norman Wright

"She expects me to have all these reactions right at my fingertips and be able to call them up on the spot. Well, I can't do that. I don't operate the way she does. I need a little more time to think things through. I don't want to say something I'm going to regret later on. Somehow she has the idea that wanting time to think is not being open and honest with her. That's ridiculous. I'm not trying to hide anything, I'm just trying to be sure in my own mind before I talk to her about it. What's wrong with that?"

"Men are just more rational than women. We prefer to deal with things in a thoughtful, rational way. Women are emotional, and that's the way they want to deal with things. Just because a man prefers to discuss things logically doesn't mean he is any less involved than a woman who wears her emotions on her sleeve. Women could profit a lot from thinking things through instead of just reacting off the top of their hearts all the time."[7]

Many of the men of our day choke when it comes to sharing tender, caring feelings with others. These men are not cruel, insensitive, noncaring individuals but they find it impossible to communicate to others the inner reservoir of emotional expression. I have talked with such men and I remember one in particular who said, "I was so proud of my wife the other day. She's been taking some art lessons and finished her painting. It was displayed in the window of the artist's studio and two people wanted to buy it for an incredible amount of money! I don't know that much about art but I thought it was great and was really feeling good about her success."

I replied, "That's great. How much of what you just shared with me did you tell her?"

He looked at me and said, "Well, I'm sure she knows how proud I am of her."

I replied, "How? How would she know that? Did you tell her what you told me? Did you tell her you were proud of her? Did you tell her you were feeling good about her success? Did you tell her you thought her art was great?"

He waited and thought and then looked up at me and said, "No, I guess I didn't. It would make a difference, wouldn't it?" I replied, "Yes, it could change her perception of you to that of a caring person if you would let her in on those inner feelings. They're a tremendous gift which she would like to receive."

Crying in Comfort?

When we were children we were frequently mocked and ridiculed for our tears. Even when a man finally realizes that crying is good and men need to cry as an expression of various emotional responses, the discomfort of it lingers for many years. When a man sees another man crying he often feels threatened, offended, wants to leave or somehow put a stop to those tears. When a man sees a woman crying, the tears bring out a protective feeling. Observing another man crying, on the other hand, often elicits uneasiness and even the response of "Why can't he control himself?"

Most men still equate manliness with being strong, composed and poised in the midst of a difficulty or crisis. It's ironic that men who are Christians have the opportunity to be freed up and experience all of their humanity by the presence of Jesus Christ in their lives and the balanced truth of the Scriptures. Yet many have the mistaken idea that Christians are to exhibit even more control and stability. Somehow being a believer means that you don't have to give expression to feelings or tears! Jesus Christ frees us to experience the heights and depths of life, from joy to pain, from sorrow to elation—and to express that emotion in whatever way we have been psychologically created. I know this. I teach it. I encourage other men to experience it. Yet, why do I at times still struggle with controlling the tears when I am deeply moved by the pain of others or the joy, or the blessings of a worship service? The old messages are still not fully erased but I am thankful I can ignore them and give expression to those inner feelings. Tears have a cleansing quality for they release the turbulence churning around inside looking for an appropriate exit. Tears are an appropriate exit. When a man cries it does not mean he is falling apart.

A friend of mine described one of his own experiences with tears which graphically depicts the inner struggle of men. Jerry's wife called him from her mother's home in Iowa to tell him that her mother had just died. His mother-in-law had been struggling with cancer for four years and his wife had flown back for her last days. Jerry received the phone call and the message which he knew was coming. This is what he said:

"I slept a couple of hours, hopped in the car, and began the 750-mile trip to Iowa. Karen had asked me to say something at the funeral, so I prepared what I would say while I wept in the car off and on all day. I can remember thinking, *If I just hold myself together and do not shed too many tears, I'll be a real strength to everyone.* When I arrived at the Lambert homestead, Karen's father came running out to meet me. Never before had we embraced, but at that moment we did, while tears of sadness rolled from our eyes.

"I can remember walking up to Myrt's bedroom with Karen and saying, 'I could just bawl my heart out.' Karen replied, 'Please do—I'd feel so much better.' She was saying, in effect, 'If you grieve over my mom's death, I'll know that you really cared for her.' With that bit of permission I let loose a second time.

"But at the funeral itself I just knew I could not let anyone down. I had to be strong. I had to do a 'professional job' and get through my part of the service. These were my in-laws, and I couldn't 'let them down.'

"From the second I walked onto the platform I felt sadness and tears welling up inside me. The minister gave some opening remarks and then it was time for me to give the obituary and a few personal remarks. I walked to the pulpit, took a deep breath, uttered one sentence, and lost it. I began to weep. Apparently, the Lord did not have in mind that I should be in control. No matter how hard I tried to fight back the tears, they burst forth. In fact, the harder I tried to hold back, the more readily they flowed. As I looked out over the pews in that little church, those tough rural men were tearing up from one end of the sanctuary to the other.

"At that moment it occurred to me that the Lord didn't want me to control my emotions. He wanted me to let go of them. For if the professional psychologist could lose it, perhaps that meant that the other men who were mourning could lose it also. Then all of a sudden I felt a mighty surge of strength well up inside me and I gave a very hopeful talk about Myrt's life and God's promises. Again, it was as if God were in control and said, 'Okay, you've shown your sadness; now give them

Feelings—The Great Male Struggle   □   **97**

some hope.' I don't believe I will ever forget the meaning I received from the events surrounding Myrt's death. I have feelings! If I express my feelings maybe others can feel freer to express their feelings. I don't have to always be in control even if I am a man."[8]

What do the men in your life believe about tears? Have you asked them? How do you feel when you see a "grown man cry"? What do you want to do? At an appropriate time ask these questions of that special man in your life and be willing to give your response to these questions as well:

What was the first time that you can remember crying?

How old were you and what did you cry about?

How did you feel when you cried as a child?

In adolescence did you increase or decrease your crying?

What were the messages you received from your parents when you cried?

What were the messages you received from your friends when you cried?

How many times have you cried in the last three years? The last year? What was it about? How did you feel? In whose presence did you cry? How did they react?

What does crying do for you now? How do you feel when you cry? What are your concerns about other men seeing you cry?

What can I do to help you when you cry in front of me?

Where Is the Love?

For centuries a nagging question has been on the hearts of women throughout the world. *Why aren't men more loving?* But men do feel love! It's the expression of love that creates the problem. Men know they are in love but again they do not always show that love. Women tend to see feelings and behavior as the same. Many act upon their feelings and the feelings are seen in their actions. If a woman is angry, she behaves in that way. If she is elated, it's expressed in her behavior. I've heard the expression that a woman's behavior is an open window to her emotions. If this is accurate, when a man does not act in a loving manner, how is it interpreted? It is seen as "he doesn't have feelings of love."

The assumption is, no loving behavior, no love.

But men do not see behavior and feelings in the same way as women. The two are not linked together and are often seen as unrelated. A man's behavior can be a form of camouflage hiding his true feelings. You cannot always tell what the feelings are in a man based upon his behavior. A worried, anxious man may appear very calm; an angry man could appear happy and calm; a man in love could appear indifferent and uncaring. Then how do you know what a man is really feeling? That's a good question and hopefully we will get to an answer. Do you see why there is a problem here? Women have their own way of evaluating and determining love. Men have a different perspective and the two clash.

Men and women define love differently. All too often men confuse love with sex. For the most part they have a limited perspective on love. It is too narrow. It needs to be broadened and it can be! Men have a lot to learn from a woman's perspective. The problem is they do not want to admit this fact! It's a threat.

Women have a fuller range for love. Love to a woman involves time spent together with significant interchange. It involves personal concern for one another and empathy. I have seen men who are willing to learn new ways of expressing love to their wives. It takes time and commitment and willingness to admit there is more to learn. Remember the point: It often takes a crisis for a man to be willing to change! And crisis occurs when a person's balance or equilibrium is upset. But let's read on.

How do men respond to the complaints about their loving? Defensively. "A man who is too loving is not a man. If I'm too romantic with words and behavior, I might be considered effeminate. I don't want others to think I'm gay."

"Men are like that. Women are the way they are. So just let it be. No one is going to change."

"This is the only way men know how to love. That's the best we can do."

"I've never had any other model of how to love. My dad, friends . . . they're the same as I."

"Women don't want men to be soft. They want them to be strong. They may say they want us to be romantic and loving and all that stuff, but if given a choice, they want us to be strong, good providers and dependable."

"I'm not sure you can trust women. You open up too much and they take advantage of you."

How Women Keep Men from Sharing

It's true! I've seen it happen many times. A man finally opens up to a woman and what he reveals is discounted, shared with others, not believed, ridiculed, rejected and even laughed at by the woman. Remember, safety, acceptance and support are essential if a man is going to let down the bridge from his castle. He wants what he shares to be used for his welfare and not against him. Trust is a major issue. Listen to the responses from men and consider the validity of their concern.

There are reasons for distance occurring between a husband and wife. And the problem is brought into focus often when wives openly discuss the personal things that go on between them and their husbands. I know their husbands would really be angry if they knew their finances were being discussed, how they feel about their parents and even what they're concerned about at work. No, it's just not safe. If a husband shares, don't broadcast it to the whole world.

"I was at a party with my wife at church and she shared something it took me weeks to tell her. She was angry with me that night and she shared this as a joke and I was embarrassed. I was hurt and ticked off at her. If she shared this, what would happen if I really opened up? I don't want it used against me. No sir!"

"My wife is an expert on what is a 'feeling' and what isn't a 'feeling.' I have tried to tell her what's going on inside of me and she tells me, 'But that's not a feeling.' Where is this book she uses to tell her what's a feeling and what isn't? I feel like giving up if I'm never going to get it right."

"Yeah, I shared my feelings. And you know what happened? I'll tell you. I opened up about work and my frustrations and she said I just wanted sympathy and attention. I tried to show her some love and attention and she said, 'You must want something, like sex. You've got some other motive in mind.' I try to be what she wants and I get criticized because my motives are suspect."

"My wife tells me what I ought to be feeling. If she feels a certain way, I should feel the same way. If we watch a gripping movie, she wants me to feel what she feels. When she cries at church, she says, 'But didn't you feel the same way? How could you not feel that way about what was shared?' Women's feelings are not the only right feelings and if I have to feel the same way, it will never work. Can't two people in the same situation feel differently and with a different intensity—and even express it differently?"

That last question is an excellent one and I would give an emphatic yes to all three aspects of it. Feelings are not to be judged. Two people experience the same event in varying ways and they respond to the same joyful or tragic experience differently.

A woman does not have to resign herself to living with an unexpressive male. Becoming fatalistic is not the answer, and I'm not talking about divorcing him either. Don't listen if someone tells you, "Don't be so concerned about men not expressing their feelings. That's just the way they are!" Men may tend to be that way, but they can change. Challenges or reproaches do not work. Carefully worded invitations can work. Men do respond initially to questions which elicit factual responses. It's easier for a man to tell his wife what he does at work than how he feels about it. He can tell her how he did at sports or school when he was growing up easier than how he feels about what he did. But starting with the facts is an introduction to the feelings.

The sad news is that many men do not share their feelings. The good news is that most of them can learn to become complete. They need the presence of Jesus Christ in their lives to give them a basis for a new identity and security. But they also need you to help them in the process of opening up. A man needs to see your requests for sharing as a participation in his life, not an intrusion. He needs to see that you don't want to know his feelings so you can use them against him, but rather to become more intimately involved with him. He needs to see that your desire is not to control him but to share with him. He needs to know about the extent of your caring and that you will no longer continue to exist without experiencing his emotional side. You want him to experience the fullness of life which includes risks and threats, but also the delights and blessings that are available.

The big question is, "How do you help a man open up and share?" There are ways to accomplish this. Let's look at some suggestions in the next chapter.

7

How to Communicate with a Man

They sat across the table looking at one another, each intent upon what the other was saying. Their body language and verbal responses indicated they understood each other. They talked and listened on the same wavelength. When they finished their conversation, each was pleased since they understood and felt understood by the other.

Have you experienced conversations such as the one just described? Undoubtedly yes. But why do some of our conversations flow so well and others are more like an experience in frustration and miscommunication? The answer is neither complicated nor profound. In most situations when you have difficulty communicating, the two of you are *not speaking the same language.* You are talking as though each of you were speaking a different foreign language. *If you want to communicate with another person, speak that person's language.* The reason you feel comfortable in your communication with some individuals is that you are speaking the same language.

To get a couple's attention in counseling or in the Marriage Renewal seminars I conduct, I simply make the statement, "When you married your partner, you didn't realize it, but you married a foreigner." Then I wait a few seconds to let the statement sink in—as well as to notice their nonverbal responses. I continue. "Yes, the person you married was a foreigner. You both may be Caucasian, or Black or Asian, but you were still both raised in different homes with different parents, siblings, experiences and, in effect, a different culture. The foods you eat may be similar but they were probably prepared

103

differently. You have different meanings for your words, your tonal inflections and your volume. You may have come from a family where voices were raised most of the time, but not in an angry manner. Everyone was just loud. But your partner may have come from a home where voices were raised infrequently, and volume meant anger. These differences need to be understood and deciphered to prevent misunderstanding.

"If you are going to have the type of marriage relationship you hoped for when you married, you need to learn the different customs, culture and language of your partner."

A Couple's Conversation

Couples usually understand what I am talking about. And this holds true for interactions in the business world as well as in families. Let's listen in on a conversation between a married couple and discover what we can learn about man-woman communication from their interaction.

Jim is speaking: "Mary and I talk a lot but I end up getting frustrated. I can't understand why she doesn't understand my point of view. I share what I think with her, but from the questions she asks it's as though she wasn't even listening! And I'm standing there telling her something that is clear as anything to me. So I explain again and again. I try to make it clear and simple, but there's a limit to this . . ."

Mary interrupts him at this point: "Jim, the reason we go on and on at times is because I don't understand you and you don't seem to understand what I'm feeling. I need to know that you understand where I'm coming from and what my needs are."

"Mary," I say, "it's very important to you that Jim understand your feelings and Jim, it's important that Mary understand your perspective and the facts you are attempting to convey, right?" They both nod in agreement. "I wonder if the problem is that some of the words you use aren't in the other person's vocabulary. I wonder if you're just not speaking the other person's language."

Mary responds: "That could be the problem. It's hard to understand why we start out talking about the same topic, which is quite simple, but seem to talk past each other. In fact, part of the problem is how much we say. Jim doesn't say too much and I wish he would. I feel like a dentist at times having to extract the words from him like an impacted molar! He's so brief and to the point with what he says. I feel like I'm talking to Western Union and just received a telegram. Sometimes he sounds like a newspaper reporter giving me a condensed version of the daily news. Facts. All facts! His descriptions are too barren and feelings are nonexistent. I so want to be able to communicate and feel comfortable with it. And I think Jim wants to as well."

I respond by asking, "Then what is it going to take for the two of you to communicate so that you understand each other?"

That is the question for you to answer as well. What is it going to take for you to communicate with the men in your life? It's simple. Speak their language!

Let's go back to the counseling session and listen in on what transpired.

"Jim and Mary—you're struggling with a problem that most couples face. It's important that we learn not only to speak the same language but also to make sure we mean the same thing with our words. I have run into so many couples who are irritated and upset in their marriages because of such a simple matter as having different definitions for their words. You know, two people can speak Spanish and not mean the same thing. We're sitting here speaking English and using similar words, but we might have different meanings. Your experiences in life, your mind set, what you intend, can give meaning to your words. Jim, your wife might ask, 'Can we stop at the store for a minute on our way home? I'll just be a minute.' You might take the word minute literally but had better not because years of experience may have taught you we're talking about 15–20 minutes." They both grin and nod their heads in understanding.

"Jim, has Mary ever said to you, 'Jim, could I talk to you for a minute about something?' and you said yes, assuming she meant a minute but you're still discussing the issue forty minutes later?" They both nod and Jim breaks in quickly.

"Last night. That very thing happened last night. Mary, you wonder why I was getting uptight. We went on and on!"

"Well, it *was important,*" Mary says. "Did it matter that much how long it went on? You agreed we needed to talk about it and I had been feeling that way for some time."

Jim responds, "But it wasn't all right. I thought it would be since you said a minute. Warn me next time and maybe I can handle it better!"

Mary replies with a bit more feeling: "But there are many times when I feel you do have a time limit on our conversations. I almost sense that you're impatient and want to get to the bottom line. You don't want to hear all my reasons or feelings. In fact, I wish you would share more details with me. I wear a new outfit and ask you how it looks and all you say is, 'It looks fine.' Can't you tell me any more about how you feel about it? Give me some sentences instead of one or two words."

Jim looks at me and rolls his eyes and then looks at Mary and says emphatically, "But I said it looked fine. What else do you want to hear?"

I interrupt Jim and say, "On a scale of 0–10 with 0 meaning it looks terrible, like it's a discard, and a 10 meaning it's outstanding, where does the word 'fine' fall?"

"Oh," Jim says, "it's somewhere between an 8 and a 10."

Mary looks surprised and blurts out, "How would *I* know that? That's the first I've heard that fine had any meaning at all! You use the word all the time for food, the weather . . ."

"This is what I mean," I interrupt, "when I say you need to define your words. Jim, if you couldn't use the word fine and had to give a three-line description of the dress Mary is wearing right now, what would you say?"

Jim looks at Mary, smiles a little, and then says, "I like the dress. The color is good with your coloring. The dress looks like you, and I like some of the detail around the waist. It fits well and I like the curves. It just seems to look like you. And the style is flashy."

I turn to Mary, "How do you feel about Jim's response?" She smiles. "That really feels good. He really seemed to notice details and I enjoyed hearing his description. I would like this kind of response for many areas."

"I could do that," Jim says, "but when I'm with some business associates and we say 'fine' we know what we mean."

"I can understand that, Jim," I counter. "When you're

with them you speak the same language, but when you're with Mary you need to speak her language. She wants more detail, more description, more adjectives. That's what registers with her. This is a good example of what I mean by speaking the other person's language. And now that we're talking about it, which one of you tends to give more detail when you talk?" I look back and forth between them and both point at Mary and smile. "I'm the detail person," Mary says. "And quite often Jim asks me to get to the point and give him the bottom line so he understands what I'm talking about. But I just want to make sure that he's going to grasp what I'm sharing. I've always given a lot of detail and feelings, but sometimes it's like he doesn't hear my feelings. He ignores them."

Jim responds as he leans forward and looks at Mary. "I don't ignore what you are saying. I do see what you are getting at, but I don't always know what to do with those feelings. And I don't always mind the detail even though I don't need it all. But I wish you would give me the bottom line first instead of going around the barn several times and then telling me what you're talking about. I like it straightforward and to the point. Then I can handle the elaborate stuff."

"Jim," I say, "you want Mary to communicate with you like a newspaper article and then you can see what she is saying."

"A newspaper article?" Jim asks. "I'm not sure I understand."

"Most newspaper articles are structured like a pyramid," I continue. "The first sentence is a complete summary statement of what is in the article. Next comes a brief paragraph with some of the most significant summary items expanded. The final larger portion of the article will contain the minute details."

"That's exactly it," Jim says. "That makes sense to me. I can follow that approach a lot better and (he turns to Mary) I would be willing to hear some more of the detail. But I don't think I need to hear as much detail as you enjoy hearing. I don't want a two-line news summary of what you say but a *Reader's Digest* condensed version would be helpful." Fortunately for all of us, they can laugh at that.

"Jim," I say, "you're asking Mary to condense some of the details a bit and identify the bottom line right at the start. That

helps you focus on her conversation better. Is that accurate?"
He nods. "But that also means, Jim, since she enjoys detail, that when you share with her you will give her more detail than you do now. Can you handle that?" He says yes.

"Now, does my statement about marrying a foreigner make more sense to you?"

They both say, "Yes, definitely!"

The Cost of Communicating

The above is a simple illustration of what I mean by speaking another person's language. Listen to the phrases, the words, the amount of detail, the amount of content the other person expresses. Find out the meaning of the words and above all, discover how the man in your life would like you to communicate with him. The entire process of speaking the other person's language is the theme of a book which I would encourage you and the important men in your life to read. It is my *Energize Your Life through Total Communication* (published by Fleming H. Revell).

The words a man uses are a significant clue for you to use in communicating with him. You and I have three main senses—hearing, seeing and feeling. People give away their dominant sense preference by the words they use. Most of us prefer one sense over the other two for perceiving life, storing up our experiences and making decisions. The language a person uses lets you know which he prefers and what you need to use in talking with him. An auditorally oriented person tends to depend upon spoken words for his information. A visually oriented individual depends upon his eyes to perceive the world around him and uses visual images in remembering and thinking. A feeling or kinesthetically oriented person tends to feel his way through his experiences.

If the man in your life is not responding to you when you talk to him—or he appears confused—you may not be using his language. Listen to him and identify which words he uses. If you ask, "Jim, how do you feel about this?" and feeling words do not seem to register or provoke a response, try again. "How does this sound to you, Jim?" He may do it if he is an auditory preference person. If that doesn't work you

could ask, "Does this idea look all right to you?" if you sense
that he is visually oriented.

Visual people use terms like:

I see what you're saying.

That looks good to me.

I'm not too clear on this right now.

This is still a bit hazy to me.

Boy, when they asked that question, I just went blank.

That sheds a new light on the problem.

Do you pick up my perspective?

Auditory people use terms like:

That rings a bell with me.

It sounds real good to me.

I hear you.

I'm trying to tune in to what you're saying.

Listen to this new idea.

I had to ask myself.

Now, that idea is clicking with me.

Kinesthetic people use words like:

I can't get a handle on this.

I've got a good feeling about this project.

Can you get in touch with what I'm saying?

It's easy to flow with what they're saying.

I don't grasp what you're trying to do.

This is a heavy situation.

Therefore when you talk with them you may want to use sentences like:

Visual questions and statements:

It appears to you . . .

You see it in this way . . .

Do you see it that way . . . ?

How does it appear to you?

Auditory questions and statements:

Listening to you it seems as if . . .

I really hear you saying . . .

What would you like to express to her?

I kind of hear you saying that . . .

Kinesthetic questions and statements:
You are sort of feeling that . . .
You are communicating a sense of . . .
I somehow sense that you feel . . .
Are you saying that this makes you feel . . . ?

Begin to listen for the man's use of words and how he reacts to others. How does he like information presented to him? Some men have expressed to me, "It's not that I don't want to talk when I get home, but it seems like I'm hit by a steamroller when I walk in the door and one idea after another is thrown at me before I have a chance to handle the first one. I need a few minutes to unwind and then I can respond. But I prefer one issue at a time so I can ask some questions and consider what we're talking about. I don't like to be pressed for a decision immediately or have to juggle five subjects at the same time." A sensitive wife will pick up on such valuable information that her husband may share with her and follow his guidelines. And she *will* discover a difference in their communication.

What we sometimes perceive as resistance on a man's part may not be resistance at all. We're just speaking the wrong language and we need to change. Sometimes it helps to ask people how they would like the information presented. They will appreciate your sensitivity and willingness to learn their language.

A man approached me once and said, "Norm, I would like to go over this new program with you and I can do it in two ways. I can let you see it first and read over the summary pages and then ask me questions, or I can sit down with you and explain it to you step by step. Which would you prefer?" Since I tend more toward being visual and like the newspaper style initially, I read the prospectus and then asked questions.

A sales representative approached me one day and said, "Norm, I have this new testing program you've just got to hear about. I have been looking forward to telling you all about it so you can really get a feel for what we're going to be doing." I wasn't as positive about this person's approach. But someone else from the same company called later and said, "Norm, I've been wondering if you would be interested in learning about our new program. You might want to see where it is going. I can do two things. I can give you a brief three-minute summary over the phone and then you can let me know how it looks to you and we can proceed in more detail. Or I can go through the entire program step by step. Which would you prefer?" He spoke my language by using my terminology and giving me a choice.

Four Social Styles

Let's illustrate this from a little different perspective. Robert and Dorothy Bolton have written a helpful book in which they discuss four different social styles. These are patterns of interpersonal behaviors and none is better or worse than the others. Our English-speaking population in this country is fairly well divided among the four styles. Each of us has a dominant style and this can be determined by observable behaviors.

The *analytical style* combines a high level of emotional control with a low level of assertiveness. These individuals like to take a precise, deliberate and systematic approach to their work. They are the data-gatherers who like to evaluate before taking action. These people are usually industrious, well organized and objective. Do you fall into this category? Which men in your life fit this style?

The *amiable person* has a low level of assertiveness but higher than average responsiveness. Sympathetic to the needs of others, these people are able to sense what lies beneath their surface behavior. An amiable person tends to use empathy and understanding in relationships with others. He has a high level of trust in other people. Do you fall into this category? Which men in your life fit in this area?

The *expressive style* tends to be the more flamboyant. These people are high in emotional expressions and assertiveness. They like to see the overall picture, run risks to obtain their dreams and take novel approaches to problems. They enjoy life, have fun and can charm and persuade others. They tend to decide and act quickly. Do you fall into this category? Which men in your life fit this style?

Drivers are the last style. They have a high degree of

assertiveness and a high level of emotional self-control. They know what they want and where to go. They are task-oriented and get to the point quickly. They want results, and are pragmatic and decisive, competitive and independent. Do you fall into this category? Which men in your life fit this style?

Your basic social style and that of the men in your life won't change. But you can emphasize the strengths of your style, use the strengths of other styles while remaining who you are and develop flexibility to respond to other styles.[1]

How do you do this? Quite easily. The Boltons talk about style flex. This is another variation of learning to speak another person's language. Style flex is simply accenting the behaviors you have in common with another person. Simply stated, it means adding some responses you don't usually use in order to speak and respond in a way the other person understands. It also means subtracting a few you typically use to which the other person may have difficulty relating. You are moving toward the other person's style and a bit away from your own style.

If you are a driver, you have a tendency to be fast-paced and goal-oriented. These traits may make other people feel pressured. Listen to the ideas and suggestions from your man and endeavor to see things from his perspective. Try to capture his perspective and feelings. To see life through the eyes of another we need to *listen*. Since over 50 percent of what others communicate is expressed nonverbally, listen with your *eyes*. Listen with *empathy* to be able to see the situation and feel it from their perspective. Rather than agreeing with them, you are trying to experience life from their perspective which is what Romans 12:15 is all about. Listen with *openness*.

Three hindrances to effective listening are defensive listening, selective listening and filtered listening. Listen to your man as though you were an anthropologist and imagine he is from another country or planet. Try to understand this foreigner. Listen to all that is being shared *without judgment*. Listen with awareness. Compare his verbal expressions with his nonverbal signals. Sometimes the two are not in harmony and by responding to the nonverbal, you encourage him to open up even more.

"You seem to be pacing around as though something is wrong. I know you just said you were all right, but I wonder if something else is on your mind."

"The frown on your face tells me you have something on your mind. If you would like to share it, I'd be happy to listen." Proverbs 18:13 and James 1:19 are excellent guides for listening.

But what if you're working for a driver or married to one? How do you communicate with that person? It is important to make good use of the person's time. Be specific and clear in what you say, and above all keep it short. Overexplaining, rambling or not knowing what you want to say beforehand will frustrate the person and you'll lose his attention. Drivers tend to be results-oriented, so focus upon that and give the man options so he can make choices. They like to hear the plus and minus or the pros and cons of situations. Remember that a driver tends to be a bit more dominant in his left-brain style and in his own mind will be asking, "What's the point of this? What's practical? How can I use it now?"

Before we go on, let me respond to the questions I know are being raised. "Why should I have to do all the changing? Why can't I be me and communicate the way I am? Why do I have to accommodate the other person so much?" Excellent questions which deserve an answer. You do not have to deny your individuality. You can be you. And you don't have to do all the changing. You are simply making a few changes so that you and the other person can communicate better. You are not denying your basic style or way of sharing. You are responding to the other person and by doing this he will eventually feel freer to respond to you according to the way *you* feel most comfortable. That's right. By reaching into his world first, in time that person will be willing to reach into your world and adapt himself to you. He will be more open to listening to you and responding to you.

Another factor is that the greater your flexibility and adaptability, the greater the influence, effect and control you have. The person who has more ways of adapting and being flexible has more control than others! Think about it. Now, let's consider another style.

Restrain

If you tend to be expressive, the key word in communicating with others is *restrain*. Often your tendency is to make quick, impulsive decisions based on hunches. This may rattle and threaten others who are either more fact-oriented or less risk-oriented than you. Your energy level, amount of talking and even volume may overwhelm others. Restrain your impulsiveness. As I have worked with men and women like this, I ask them to work out a delay system. Do not make a decision unless you write down the pros and cons of the outcome. When people ask you to do something or go somewhere, don't give an answer immediately. Always wait and tell the person you'll get back to him. This eliminates headaches and overextending yourself. Be sure you have all the facts before you make any decisions. Listen and don't override others when they are talking. Share the limelight with others. But the key word is *restrain*.

How does one respond best to an expressive person and speak his language? This person enjoys socializing and talking about opinions, people and experiences. It's all right to talk about yourself with him. He enjoys people who are fun-loving. Talk with him about his dreams and intuitions. Share with him the overall view of your concern and then you can work on plans and details. You may need to go off on tangents a bit, but be sure to come back to the main topic. Summarize any conclusions or agreements you have made with him. You may have to oversee to make sure plans are followed and details are covered. Remember this person is very much a dominant right-brain person.

Stretch

The key word for the amiable person is *stretch*. Such people tend to be somewhat slower-paced and cooperative and are quite people-oriented. But this may create some strain with another person who is more goal-oriented and moves at a faster rate. It will be important to identify some goals and achieve them. Others will appreciate knowing where you stand. Encourage others to do their best. They will appreciate your being direct and attaining results.

How can you respond to the amiable man? Above all, appear relaxed and pace yourself in a moderate fashion. Person-to-person contact is very important and small talk is not necessary. Encourage this individual to talk and ask for his opinions. Amiable people tend to lean toward right-brain dominance and they care for people. They may even tend to rescue those who are in need. When they talk to you, reflect back to them what you hear and avoid coming back with too much logic. Be patient in your communication and encourage them to express their feelings. They do not handle pressure too well and they need to feel you are walking alongside them. Therefore, set goals together even if you suggest them. Such people like your cooperative support. Occasionally they may need you to make sure they carry out their responsibilities. Minimize the risk factor of decisions or new ventures, as risk is difficult for them. They also need to be able to trust your assurances. Amiable men need more ongoing contact than the other styles.

Decide

If you are an analytical person, your key word is *decide.* It's one thing to be thorough and gather facts, but at some point decisions need to be made. When you're involved in a discussion with a man, it is healthy to take a stand during the discussion phase. As you consider alternatives, don't hinder others who work more rapidly. Make decisions and act. You will probably discover that you make decisions just as well as you did when you took more time.

In responding to this style, remember that analyticals are very much left-brain dominant. They may tend to be skeptical and evaluate and critique. Pace yourself in a moderate way with them—they like to know what it is you're talking about. In approaching a person such as this be sure you are prepared, factual, logical but not overly sterile and businesslike. They like to hear the pros and cons of a proposition from you. This shows them you have thought it out. They need to be shown the low risk level of what you are proposing. Overstatements are not trusted by the analytical, so don't exaggerate. If you use words like "never," "always," "all," "everyone" and so on, you will be challenged or not believed. Allow this person to proceed in a deliberate fashion, but if he is too indecisive, encourage him along. But do not make his decisions for him. It's good to put any conclusions down in writing or put them on the calendar to act as a reminder.

I hope you're not overwhelmed by all of this, but if so go back and reread this section. Be sure to read the book, *Energize Your Life through Total Communication.* If this sounds like a lot of work, it will be for a while. But if the way you are communicating isn't really working, what have you got to lose? Learning to speak another's language will help you with men in any situation as well as with women.

I'm often asked, "Norm, if you had just one book to recommend on communication, what would it be?" My answer takes no thought or time, since there is one which stands far above all other books. If men and women would follow the communication guidelines of that book, we wouldn't have the difficulties we do. The Bible is the finest guide we have for communication. Our application of these principles needs to be sensitive and we do need to adapt to the other people in our lives. But consider this sampling of verses from the Amplified Bible. For each one, identify how you will put this passage into practice as you communicate with that man in your life.

• *Proverbs 25:11* A word fitly spoken and in due season is like apples of gold in a setting of silver.

• *Proverbs 15:4, 23* A gentle tongue [with its healing power] is a tree of life, but willful contrariness in it breaks down the spirit . . . . A man has joy in making an apt answer, and a word spoken at the right moment, how good it is!

• *Ephesians 4:15* Rather, let our lives lovingly express truth in all things—speaking truly, dealing truly, living truly . . . .

• *Proverbs 18:13* He who answers a matter before he hears the facts, it is folly and shame to him.

• *James 1:19* Let every man be quick to hear, a ready listener, slow to speak, slow to take offense and to get angry.

• *Proverbs 16:32* He who is slow to anger is better than the mighty, and he who rules his own spirit than he who takes a city.

• *Proverbs 14:29* He who is slow to anger has great

understanding, but he who is hasty of spirit exposes and exalts his folly.

● *Ephesians 4:31* Let all bitterness and indignation and wrath . . . and resentment . . . and quarreling . . . and slander be banished from you, with all malice.

● *Romans 14:13* Then let us no more criticize and blame and pass judgment on one another, but rather decide and endeavor never to put a stumbling block or an obstacle or a hindrance in the way of a brother.

● *Proverbs 12:16* A fool's wrath is quickly and openly known; but a prudent man ignores an insult.

● *Proverbs 28:13* He who covers his transgressions will not prosper, but whoever confesses and forsakes his sins shall obtain mercy.

● *Proverbs 10:19* In a multitude of words transgression is not lacking, but he who restrains his lips is prudent.

● *Proverbs 21:19* It is better to dwell in a desert land than with a contentious woman and vexation.

● *1 Thessalonians 5:11* Therefore encourage one another and edify—strengthen and build up—one another just as you are doing.

8

Helping Men Share Their Feelings

If you are looking for guaranteed answers and solutions, don't read on! If you are looking for some basic ideas and suggestions that others have been willing to try, *then read on.* There is a risk involved in helping a man share his feelings, but the benefits that can occur outweigh the risk. You will need to take into consideration the uniqueness of the man in your life and adapt any suggestions to his situation. You will also need to modify any suggestions given here which will necessitate some thinking and prayer. Remember some basic principles about a man's response.

A man may be willing to share himself and his feelings more if some of his fears and myths about sharing are eliminated. A man (whether he admits it or not) fears the risks involved in disclosure. He would like all risks to be lifted, but that is an unrealistic expectation. It will always be a risk to open up and venture into a new arena of life. He won't believe it if you tell him there are no risks. It is far better to convince him that whatever reduced risks still exist, he will be able to handle them. It might be helpful to say, "I understand that this is difficult to share, but I would like to help you through this uncomfortable time, not hinder you."

Men who do change and become more open often attribute their change to the assistance of another person. If a man can handle some minor risks and learn to be comfortable, he will be encouraged to open up even more. As you endeavor to build intimacy with your man, trust must also be rebuilt.

Some men will hesitate to share because the myth they

have concerning emotional intimacy is, "I must be open with everyone all of the time." If they are uncertain what to share and with whom, they feel better not sharing at all. Your man doesn't have to share with everyone nor all the time with you.

Remember that you are asking another person to change his way of responding to life. Is this right? Aren't we just to accept others as they are?

What about asking for change? Can the Word of God shed any light on this?

How does the biblical mandate to exhort one another or encourage one another apply to the desire for change? Let's look at some examples from the Word of God.

"And when [Apollos] wished to cross to Achaia [most of Greece], the brethren wrote to the disciples there, urging and encouraging them to accept and welcome him heartily" (Acts 18:27).

"I entreat and advise Euodia and I entreat and advise Syntyche to agree and to work in harmony in the Lord" (Philippians 4:2).

"Let the word [spoken by] the Christ, the Messiah, have its home [in your hearts and minds] and dwell in you in [all its] richness, as you teach and admonish and train one another in all insight and intelligence and wisdom [in spiritual things, and sing] psalms and hymns and spiritual songs, making melody to God with [His] grace in your hearts" (Colossians 3:16).

"But we beseech and earnestly exhort all you, brethren, that you excel [in this matter] more and more" (1 Thessalonians 4:10).

Who determines what we are to exhort another person to do? Who determines what we are to teach or encourage another person to do?

The word exhort in these passages means to urge one to pursue some course of conduct. It is always looking to the future. Exhorting one another is a threefold ministry in which one believer urges another to action in terms of applying scriptural truth, encourages the person with scriptural truth and comforts the person through the application of scripture. To "encourage" is to urge forward or persuade in Acts 18:27. In 1 Thessalonians 5:11 it means to stimulate another to the ordinary duties of life. Therefore, what are we to exhort another person to do? Does the expression of feelings fall into this category?

Personally, I think so. There is more to life than being emotionally repressed regardless of the reason. God created each one of us as emotional beings, and life is much richer when we experience our emotions. The intensity and expression will vary. If a man chooses to isolate himself and not have in-depth interpersonal relationships, there may be no impetus to change. But whenever there is a close man-woman relationship (especially marriage), for intimacy to occur, feelings must be part of the relationship.

What you believe about feelings and emotions will affect what you request and how you respond to a man. Plan a time to ask these questions of your man or invite him to respond in writing.

Take some paper and write down your answers to the following questions.

1. Do I feel it's all right to express my feelings and emotions and to talk about them? Do I feel that feelings and emotions are bad? How would the man in my life answer these questions?

2. Do I allow my emotions to emerge within me naturally without trying to push them down? Do I feel I have to fake emotions that I don't feel to please others—or because I think I should feel this way? How would this man answer these questions?

3. Are there any emotions that I overdo, and if so what are they? Are there emotions that I refuse to show or allow to be demonstrated in my presence? Which emotions does this man show that bother me?

4. Do I let my emotions enter into my speech and communication, or is there too much control? Do I know how to put feelings into words? Does this man?

5. Do I use my emotions to get what I want or to cause others to leave me alone? Does this man? Which emotions are used?

6. Do I talk about my emotions when they arise or do I wait until another time when I might feel safer? Does the man in my life do so? Which emotions do I express immediately and which do I delay?

7. True or false. I believe I have the right to express any of my emotions at any time as long as I don't step on the rights of others. Do I ever violate the rights of others by the use of my emotions? Do I feel that this man does?

8. Am I willing to take risks in expressing my emotions? Do I still express them if others become upset or blame me for the problem that is being created? Can I express emotions without losing control? Can this man? Describe a time when you expressed your anger in a healthy way.

9. How do I feel when others are expressing their emotions? Have I ever or do I usually try to get others not to express their emotions? Am I a feeling-stopper?

10. Which emotions are the most difficult for me to express? How can this man help me in expressing these? Which emotions are the most difficult for this man to express?

Expressing Your Feelings

Many people have difficulty expressing certain types of feelings. Here are some of those feelings. Let's see how you would deal with these issues. Take each topic listed here and write what you would say to express this feeling. If your man feels like this, what does he do to express this feeling? Could he be expressing it already and you're not catching it? Think about it.

Feelings about not being able to do things;
Feelings about not being able to change a situation;
Feelings of jealousy;
Feelings of not being able to handle compliments or affection;
Feelings of being hurt or rejected;
Feelings of wanting to punish someone;
Feelings of guilt or a need to be punished;
Feelings of shame;
Feelings of helplessness;
Feelings of disappointment;
Feelings of depression;
Feelings of being a worthwhile person and valued by others;
Feelings of being inadequate.

11. How do I feel about myself? Are my feelings positive or negative? How do I feel about others? These feelings toward

myself or others, and how they are expressed, will affect my emotional life.[1]

After you and the other person have worked through this list, plan a time to talk with him about these feelings. Ask him to describe them. Take some blank pieces of paper and crayons and draw (literally or symbolically) how that person feels when he experiences this emotion. Share your picture with one another and then verbally describe the feelings. This allows people to think about their feelings and helps them put their feelings into words. Here are some examples of basic feeling words:

Embarrassed	Guilty	Depressed
Loving	Affectionate	Afraid
Worried	Fearful	Frustrated
Helpful	Hurt	Joyful
Jealous	Inferior	Lonely
Accepted	Rejected	Defensive
Disappointed	Sad	Shy
Trustworthy	Mistrusted	Angry

Another way of helping a person express his feelings is to use a sentence-completion form and make a game of finishing the sentences. Here are some examples. You can probably think of others that would be interesting for your own situation. Each person should share the first response that comes to mind without thinking a long time about what he will say.

I like myself best when . . .
I feel upset about myself when . . .
I get angry at _____ when . . .
I get angry with myself when . . .
When I do something right I feel . . .
When I fail I feel . . .
I feel good when . . .
I feel bad when . . .
I feel happy when . . .
I feel sad when . . .
I am scared when . . .
I feel safe when . . .[1]

Make Positive Requests

To help a person change, you must have some kind of a plan in mind. First of all, you will have to decide if you can become comfortable with these approaches and then pray, think and plan how to apply them to your area of concern. Be sure to approach the man in a style that is easiest for him. Be sure that you speak his language. (Refer to the chapter on how to communicate with a man.)

The first thing you need to do is to make a request. You may feel that, "I've tried all this before," but have you really? Too often requests are stated or come across as demands. The intensity and tone of voice may carry the real message that you're feeling.

When you make a request, keep it specific and positive, not negative and general. Going to your partner and saying, "You're so inconsiderate," or "You're never affectionate," does little to promote change. But saying, "I would really appreciate it if, when you come home, you would come up to me, put your arm around me, and ask how my day was," or "It really makes my day when you put your things away when you come home." Point to the desired behavior rather than pointing out what's lacking. It also conveys the belief that the other person is capable of changing.

Within a Request—Do the Following

First of all, you must give the person information. Each person has a different need for and capacity for handling information. For most individuals, the more information you provide about a desired change the less the resistance. Why? Because there is more opportunity for him to see the request for change as a step toward growth. "John, I appreciate your interest in my work and my daily tasks. I'd like you to help me sort through my feelings about what is going on. It would help me to know how you feel about what I've shared. This would help me a great deal. I know it will take some time, but both what you think and how you feel are important to me. And that will help me to make some of the decisions that I've been putting off."

Involving the partner in exploring various alternatives for change will also lessen resistance. Your man will be less defensive if he has a chance to express his ideas and make suggestions. "John, you know that we've been able to talk a bit more lately about how the home is kept and also our scheduling difficulties. I'm wondering if we could explore some possible alternatives that might work. This doesn't mean we're going to just accept whatever idea is shared, but just that we get some more ideas to work with. What do you think?"

Start out slowly so that the request is easier to respond to. Is the change requested an overwhelming and gigantic step? Or have you broken the request down into small increments which can actually be accomplished? If so, there may be better response. If the requested change is for increased communication, starting out sharing for fifteen minutes one night a week is reasonable. Your goal may be thirty minutes a night, four nights a week, but that may be too much to expect at first. Sharing a few feelings from the past—or less threatening feelings—may be easier. Show that you believe the other person is capable of changing.

Intimacy is a final factor. Resistance is a normal response when one person mistrusts and fears the other. If motives or intentions are questioned, how can a suggested change be seen as anything but damaging? If trust and intimacy exist, a spouse may see the request as one way to achieve even greater intimacy in the marriage. For example, a husband who has responded favorably to his previous suggestions for change will be open if:

1. His wife acknowledges his change in a positive way. She doesn't say, "Well, it won't last," or "It's about time," or "I can't believe it."

2. She doesn't mention his change or lack of change in front of others to embarrass him.

3. He is open to change himself.

4. He knows she loves him whether he changes or not.

5. He sees her request for change as something that will enhance his life. It needs to be presented in this manner.

What can a wife do to help her husband share his feelings?

A wife can do a number of things to help her husband become more expressive, but the changes, if they do occur, will take time. You are battling years of conditioning, so beware of making demands or setting a timetable that he cannot meet as yet.

Barbara, a forty-year-old mother and accountant, said, "When I wanted John to share, I wanted his feelings when I wanted them. My requests came across as demands. And one day he told me so. I learned to be sensitive to his days and moods, and whenever he began to share some of his frustrations I listened and listened well. He didn't want a dialogue or someone to solve his problem. He wanted to vent, and I wanted to hear!"

Some of the suggestions that follow may sound familiar, others quite new. Remember, if what you're doing now isn't working, why keep using the same approach? A new approach used in a loving, consistent manner may help build the intimacy you're looking for.

Help your husband acknowledge he has feelings inside of him, and that by learning to share these your relationship will bloom. One husband said, "After fifteen years of marriage, I wondered why our relationship was so stale. And then I realized it wasn't the relationship, it was me! When Jan asked me questions or wanted to talk, I gave her thoughts and facts, but no feelings. She could have gotten the same from a computer. We decided to take fifteen minutes a day to share. She agreed to summarize her three-minute descriptions into three or four lines. I agreed to share whatever I said with feeling words. It took us a while to learn this new style, but what a difference it has made! I share—she listens—and we feel closer."

What if you ask the man in your life to share more of his feelings and he responds with, "I just don't know how. If I knew how then I would"? If you respond with, "Well, it's not so hard. Just start sharing them," don't expect much of a response. He just doesn't know how and he needs some help. A better response would be, "I appreciate you letting me know this. I can understand how frustrating that could be. If you'd like some suggestions, let me know." And wait to see if he responds.

Do not hound him if there is no response at this time. If he doesn't pick up on your offer, you may want to mention it one more time. When he does respond be sure you have something to offer. You might say, "You know, a lot of men and women just never had the opportunity to develop a feelings vocabulary. I've heard of some people who get a book like a collection of synonyms and antonyms and then they can look up different words to expand their vocabulary." For your own personal use (and perhaps you could even share this list with him) here is a list of eight different feeling words with their amplification:

Hate	Fear	Anger	Happiness
1. dislike	1. fright	1. sore	1. joyful
2. bitter	2. terror	2. offended	2. enthusiastic
3. hateful	3. anxious	3. mad	3. merry
4. odious	4. misgivings	4. resentful	4. lucky
5. detest	5. concern	5. wrathful	5. fortunate
6. spiteful	6. harassed	6. hostile	6. pleased
7. aversion	7. dread	7. displeased	7. glad
8. despise	8. alarm	8. injured	8. satisfied
9. loathe	9. apprehension	9. vexed	9. contented
10. abominate	10. worry	10. torment	10. delighted

Love	Disappointment	Sadness	Confusion
1. affection	1. disturbed	1. fearful	1. mixed-up
2. loving	2. unhappy	2. grief	2. doubtful
3. amorous	3. dissatisfied	3. dejected	3. disorder
4. likable	4. frustrated	4. torment	4. bewilderment
5. tenderness	5. deluded	5. anguish	5. confounded
6. devotion	6. defeated	6. sorrow	6. disarray
7. attachment	7. hurt	7. unhappy	7. jumble
8. fondness	8. failure	8. gloomy	8. uncertain
9. passion	9. rejection	9. melancholy	9. perplexed
10. endearing	10. thwarted	10. mournful	10. embarrassment

You might also say, "When you tell me a fact or a thought, perhaps you could add, 'and I feel . . .' It may feel strange and uncomfortable at first or you may not even know how to put it into words and that's all right. If you would like me to help you try to describe it, I'd be glad to help. But you let me know if you want me to."

You could suggest that he try to name the feeling, or use a simile or metaphor. If we don't have enough labels to describe our emotions, we can use these. "I feel squelched" or "I feel like a cool breeze blowing through the air" or "I felt so bad at work today, it seemed like a herd of elephants ran over me and I'm part of the pieces."

A man can try to put into words what response or action his feelings prompt him to show! "I was so angry I felt like kicking the dog," or "I felt so happy I wanted to hug my car when it finally arrived."

Figures of speech can help: "The sun was really shining on me today" or "I felt like God didn't even exist today."

Try straightforward questions that encourage a direct response.

"I'd like to know the most interesting experience you had at work today (or this week)."

"When have you felt angry, sad, excited, happy or whatever this week—and what caused it?"

"I feel there's a portion of you I don't know. If I had to describe how you feel about your work, what would I say?"

"You really seem to enjoy your woodworking. What do you enjoy so much about it?"

"When you were a little boy, what were your greatest delights and your greatest fears?"

By asking thought-provoking questions about topics fairly comfortable to him—like work, hobby, childhood—you make it easier for your man to communicate. These questions vary in their degree of comfort for him. Sometimes it's easier to pose a factual question first, then lead into how he feels about it. Most husbands find it easy to describe facts about work. But it may take a man time to discuss the joys, frustrations or boredom of his job.

One wife asked her husband: "Honey, you know I enjoy hearing more details and feelings from you. Often it appears that you seem hesitant to talk to me about them. Is there something I do to make it difficult for you to share these with me?"

Another wife was more direct: "John, you know I like to hear the details, your feelings, the inner workings of who you are. I need this, and the times you have shared with me were fantastic. You're so articulate and have such depth. You probably feel I pressure you—or even nag you—into opening up to me. I know you don't like it when I do slip into that trap. I want you to know that I'm not trying to nag. But I do appreciate your sharing more with me."

Some men respond to admissions of "I've been there before" or "I've had difficulty when I've experienced this or tried that." Telling or sharing a story of what has happened to you may enable the other person to begin talking. Admitting your own concerns may enable the other person to open up to his own inner feelings.

Allow a man to share his feelings in his own manner. He doesn't always have to be serious to begin with or sit there holding your hands, talking intently about the inner "depth of his being." Some men are more relaxed when they can tell it their way. Allow the man to feel in charge of how he shares his feelings. The way you receive a man's feelings will determine what happens in the future. If a man shares a problem he has had at work, he does not want to hear a response like, "What did you do to bring that about?" Or he may not even want to problem solve at that time. A man who comes from a background where blame and criticism were constantly given may have to be convinced that you are for and not against him.

Develop an atmosphere of trust so he will eventually be able to express the entire gamut of feelings arising in him. If you ask your husband how he feels about his job and he says he hates it and wants to quit, your own feelings of insecurity may cause you to respond, "You can't! Think of us and our children!" And your husband won't be as open with you again. You don't have to agree with his feelings; the goal is not to debate, but to build communication and thus intimacy.

Thank him for sharing. Let him know how much it means to you and ask if there's anything you can do to make it easier for him. Before he leaves for work in the morning, ask what it is that you can pray about for him that day. This gives you something specific to talk about at the end of the day.

Often watching a movie together can open the emotional side of a person. A film can bring out feelings in a person who would ordinarily suppress them. Emotions brought to the surface through the film seem "safe" because in a sense they are not "real." Discussing the movie later, using factual and feeling questions, may lead to unique discussion.

What then is the answer to some of the complaints and

concerns which men and women bring up about one another? The answer is, adjust, change and reinforce any changes which occur.

Before you talk with your spouse about sharing feelings, there are several steps you need to take. First of all, you need prayerfully to consider what to say and spend quantities of time seeking God's direction in prayer. Secondly, it may be helpful to discuss what to do with a qualified person who believes in this approach. Thirdly, spend time writing down the typical ways you respond to your spouse's comments, including the specific statements you make. Then write out and rehearse aloud what you are going to say instead. Try to anticipate your spouse's response so you can prepare yourself for his or her reply.

The Broken Record Technique

Be sure you are familiar with the use of the broken record technique in case you need to use this. It has proven to be very effective. The broken record technique is simply saying over and over again what you want without becoming angry, obnoxious, irritated, loud or out of control. You stick to your point as though you were a record with the needle stuck. You ignore all side issues which are brought up and also disregard a request for reasons behind the confrontation ("Why are you doing this to me?"). You are not thrown by what the other person says and you continue to be persistent. Listen to this conversation:

Betty: Ken, I've been concerned recently about our communication and I thought it might help a bit to talk about it.

Ken: Oh, good grief. There you go again, griping about something in our marriage. It seems like you've always got some complaint.

Betty: I can understand why you might feel that way, but I am concerned about our communication and the sharing of our feelings and would like to talk about it.

Ken: Well, I communicate the way I do and I don't see any problem with it. Your way of talking isn't always the best and you give an overload of emotions and feelings. You give enough for both of us.

Betty: You could be right about how many feelings I share and I will work on that. I am concerned, however, about our communication style and thought it would be good for us to talk some about it.

Ken: What's to talk about? We talk and I know how you feel.

Betty: Ken, I am concerned about our communication and how you feel and I would really like to hear more of your feelings just as you're doing right now.

Ken: (Sighs) Well, what about my feelings? Go on.

When you are repetitive and persistent, the other person often realizes that he or she is not going to sidetrack you and perhaps reluctantly begins to discuss the issue.

I have found helpful, specific suggestions on this subject and dialogue in *When I Say No I Feel Guilty* by Manuel Smith (Bantam).

Paula and Rex

Paula and Rex had been married for ten years. Rex was an engineer and deeply involved with his profession and his church. From all external appearances their marriage appeared to be quite a good one. But there was little if any emotional intimacy, mainly because Rex did not know how to share his emotions and avoided expressing his feelings, especially when Paula began, as he called it, one of their "emotional discussions."

Paula was slowly starving to death emotionally and was concerned that the rest of her married life would be emotionally vacant. She pressured Rex, begged him, cried and became angry but nothing seemed to work. She wanted not only the emotional interaction but some time and attention from Rex. Out of his fear of emotional interactions with Paula Rex was becoming more and more preoccupied.

Fortunately, however, Paula began following a new approach. She began showing much more self-confidence and independence, without giving an explanation for what she was doing. Whereas before she depended heavily on Rex and asked his opinion on practically everything in her attempt to engage him in the relationship, she now reversed her approach. She scheduled some activities for herself without consulting him and was no longer the pursuer.

Rex began to share a bit more with her as the pressure on him decreased. One evening as he was talking, Paula said, "You know, I appreciate how clearly and factually you communicate with me. That's helpful to me. You're very good at sharing the facts and the logical points. In fact, much better than I am. I'm much more into emotions and that's where my skill and strengths lie. I sure can learn a lot from the way you think and communicate. I appreciate that. Some day, when you are ready and interested in learning about emotions and feelings, let me know and I think I have some new information which might amaze you. In fact, it will change a lot of your life, not only with me, but with everyone else with whom you come in contact."

With that she went into the other room and busied herself doing the dishes. She did not mention the subject again for several days. A few days later they were in a discussion and Paula asked Rex how he felt about an issue. She quickly corrected herself and said, "I'm sorry, I didn't mean to ask how you felt about that. I meant what did you think about it?"

"Wait a minute!" Rex replied. "I can handle that question about my feelings! I'm not dead, you know. And by the way, you made a statement about learning about emotions and feelings. What did you mean by that?"

"Do you really want to know?" Paula asked.

"Yes, I do," Rex said.

"Well, I appreciate that," Paula replied. "We need more time than we have tonight. Can I take you out to dinner tomorrow night where we have some privacy and enough time to talk? I have a new place picked out which serves your favorite food. How does that sound?"

Rex hesitated and said, "Well, why not now?"

Paula replied, "Let's talk tomorrow night, okay?" And they did. Rex was puzzled and intrigued by Paula's response. In a sense, he was no longer in control of the situation.

At dinner the next evening, Paula shared her love for and commitment to Rex. She also shared her need for emotional intimacy and said, "I understand I have pressured you and I am sorry for that. We both came into this marriage speaking different languages. You spoke facts, brief sentences and a lot of logic. I talked more, shared feelings and used different words. We each spoke a foreign language. I think we can both learn each other's language and have an even better relationship. What do you think?" She kept asking his opinion using his language; finally she suggested, "I have found two books which I think can make a difference. If you would like to read them, I have them for you. But if you are not ready and would like more time to consider our discussion, that would be fine. We don't have to do it now."

"Well, wait a minute," Rex said. "I would like to see what you have." Paula reached into her handbag and pulled out two books. One was *Why Am I Afraid to Tell You Who I Am?* by John Powell (Argus) and the other was *The Secrets Men Keep—Breaking the Silence Barrier* by Dr. Ken Druck and James Simmons (Doubleday). Without comment she gave both to Rex. She did not mention the books again until Rex began to talk about them. In fact, he started reading some of the pages to her. Within weeks their relationship began to improve and Rex started to discover the world of feelings and vulnerability. Fortunately, this couple's story had a positive ending. Many do, but there are other couples where either the husband or the wife is so ingrained in a particular way of living life that they may continue to retreat even with this approach. That's the risk but it is better than taking no action at all.

Do the Unexpected and Don't Be Predictable!

Keep track of what you do and what you say for several days and note the other person's response. Next, in writing, describe what you would need to do in order to be unpredictable and different. Then rehearse the new statements and map out in detail how you will use them. Try to anticipate your spouse's responses, both positive and negative. Practice. Practice. Discuss your new approach with a *trusted* friend or even a counselor. Be sure you ask yourself the question: Am I willing to change as much as I want the other person to change? One of the best ways to help another person to change is to become a pacesetter in change yourself. Philippians 3:12–14 (NASB) says:

Not that I have already obtained it, or have already become perfect, but I press on in order that I may lay hold of that for which also I was laid hold of by Christ Jesus. Brethren, I do not regard myself as having laid hold of it yet; but one thing I do: forgetting what lies behind and reaching forward to what lies ahead, I press on toward the goal for the prize of the upward call of God in Christ Jesus.

Note: I would encourage both men and women to read my book *Energize Your Life through Total Communication* (Revell). It was released the day I finished this chapter!

9

High Noon in a Man's Life

I was eating lunch by myself in a restaurant when I noticed two middle-aged men sitting at the table next to me. Our tables were separated by a short palm tree. But it wasn't too difficult to hear their conversation, which was very intense. They appeared to be close friends.

One of the men (I'll call him Jim) said to his friend, "I don't know what's wrong with me lately. I'm getting more and more indifferent about my work. What used to excite me seems boring. I don't know if it's me or my job. Sometimes I'd like to walk away from it all and move up to Wyoming to my cousin's ranch. But if I mentioned that to Jenny, she'd come apart at the seams. I can just hear her now, 'What! Give up all that we've worked for all these years! And what about the kids? And what about and what about . . . ?'"

His friend continued to listen while Jim went on. "You know what scares me about this whole thing? I'm beginning to question everything! I'm questioning my faith and I'm an elder at church. I'm questioning my relationship with Jenny and I've been married twenty-three years now. I'm asking myself some dumb questions and I can't get them out of my mind."

His friend nodded. "Could some of your questions be like, 'Do I really want to go on knocking myself out for this company for the next twenty-three years of my life? Am I really going to move up or am I stuck at this level? And if I do move up, is that what I want?' Are these some of the questions?"

Jim looked at him and replied, "Exactly. It sounds like you've been inside my head listening. But it's not only my job. At times I have questions about Jenny and me. It's become,

134

well, routine and dull. I've never been blind to the fact there are other attractive women around, but now I'm not only noticing them but sometimes thinking about them. But I still love Jenny. Part of me yearns for some changes and part of me says, 'Forget it and keep your nose to the grindstone.' It's like I'm engaging in this introspection trip and the more I look the more I find, and I feel trapped. What's wrong with me?"

"Welcome to the club," Jim's friend replied. "I went through some of the same feelings and reactions about two years ago. Perhaps not with the same intensity, but the questions were there. Fortunately, I did some reading and talked through a lot of these issues with my wife and I've got a better handle on it. Friend, you're not alone. All men go through some type of transition at this time of life. The fact that nobody warns us about it makes it a bit more threatening."

What It's Like in Midlife

I would like for you to come with me into the inner world of the man in midlife. This is the major transition time for most men and what you often see on the outside does not always tell you about his inner thoughts and feelings. Midlife has been called the "noon-time" of a man's life. For all men it's a time of transition. For some it is a time of moving from the gentle swells of a stable ocean to the rough seas. The passage is difficult before they reach solid land once again.

Middle age is the time when a man has lived half of his probable lifespan. It is a time of life which ranges anywhere from age thirty-five to the mid-fifties. It is a state of mind. A man senses the passage of time and this leads him to change his values and his view of life. This is a time when men come face to face with fulfilled and unfulfilled dreams, achievements, goals and relationships. There is a transition in thinking from "if I die" to "when I die," and this abrupt encounter with mortality can be quite traumatic. Many men look at their lives and think of the things they had hoped for and how little they feel they have accomplished. The seeds of despair begin to grow. It is a point at which men accept the end of perfectionistic illusions about themselves. You will be told about this despair, but not always directly or verbally.

Men approaching forty face the most serious transition of all. Outwardly we often laugh about it while inwardly we mourn over it. Why don't we have big birthday parties when we turn thirty as we so often do when we turn forty? The surprise birthday celebration at forty is very common but underneath the laughter and celebration may be another set of feelings which we would prefer to deny rather than face. The questions begin to emerge and no amount of repression and avoidance will make them disappear. The questions keep bursting through a man's defenses. "What if I made, or make the wrong decision about success, work, love, my children, my money? What if . . . ? What if . . . ? If only . . . . Did I aim too high or too low? Am I living my life or someone else's? What do I really want for myself and others in my life? How am I using or misusing my abilities? Am I satisfied? Can I be satisfied? Do I dare share what I am feeling? What will others think of me? What happens if I die tomorrow? What if I work for all this and don't live to enjoy it? Is this all there is to life?" Many men feel the words from Dante's *Inferno,*

> In the middle of the journey of our life,
> I came to myself in a dark wood,
> Where the right way was lost.[1]

This is a time when men live with one foot in youth and the other in maturity, and readjustment is the theme. They have to live with mixed messages about a middle-aged man's future.

This is a time to bask in public acclaim, or suffer public shame. It will be his prime time of life or the time when he feels his age. It is a time to receive respect as an authority, or it may be the time when he is perceived as a "tyrant" or "over the hill." It is a time when he can do some things for himself—or a time of extreme loneliness because his spouse is gone, the children have left and friends have died.[2]

Midlife is the time when men discover that work, wealth, fame, status, exercise, health fads and diets have all been in vain in a sense, for they cannot prevent old age, illness or death. They do not stop the wheel of time from turning. Men see their parents lowered into the grave of death, feel their own body changes and see younger people moving ahead of them and taking over. And they ask themselves, "Why?"

Many men react to the facts of life and the changes by resisting. The resistance can take many forms from avoidance and denial to moving ahead in life with blinders attached to their heads. Others become pursuers of what they feel they are losing or have never had. Many men's temptations at this time reflect false satisfactions. The big four, as they are often called, can emerge with great intensity at this point: power, sex, status and money. The pursuit of these, unfortunately, leads to emptiness which can increase the man's despair at this time of life.

Accumulating more money, dominating more people, climbing higher at work and seducing younger women does not satisfy—but they are a common pattern.

They are illusive. In fact, they increase the depth of emptiness and fail to shield a man from the necessity of coming to grips with his values. *For the crisis of midlife is a crisis of defining and redefining values.*

Joyce Brothers says that men in their forties are men of affairs, more often in fantasy than in reality, but many men do take action to satisfy their lust at this age. While at this time they are devoted to their marriages, I have worked with many of them in counseling. The affair was their attempt to deny their aging, to avoid acknowledging they are moving closer to death. For a while his outside involvement gives the man the feeling that he is young and vital again. But like aspirin, the affair provides only temporary relief. Many a man in midlife deludes himself into believing that the new woman is so much better than his wife. He does this by focusing on the lacks and negatives of his own marriage, but he fails to remember all of the positives. With the new woman there is basically only a positive experience with very little or no negatives to detract.

These are also years of great responsibility: business and family decisions, community and church responsibilities all weigh upon the person in this prime time of life. It is a time of realizing potentials and accepting limitations.

Midlife is:

- the time when a man is always thinking that in a week or two he will feel as good as ever. (Don Marquis)

- when you are too young to get Social Security and too old to get another job.
- when you're sitting at home on a Saturday night and the telephone rings and you hope it isn't for you. (Ogden Nash)
- when your old classmates are so gray and wrinkled and bald they don't recognize you. (Bennett Cerf)
- when you are warned to slow down by a doctor instead of a policeman. (Sidney Brody)
- when you want to see how long your car will last instead of how fast it will go.[3]

This is the time of the male menopause, a word that sounds absurd when applied to men. For women, the menopause means what the word signifies—the cessation of menstruation. Women lose their ability to reproduce, but men do not.

For some men it takes the better part of a decade to deal with all the emotions which emerge during midlife. Questions and feelings come and go during this time. One of the most pressing issues of midlife is to lessen the distance between what we think, how we feel, what we say and what we do.

Crisis of Uncertainty

It is important to realize that all men experience some type of transition but not all men experience a full midlife crisis. It is somewhat easy to identify in advance those who are most prone to actually experience the crisis as contrasted to a simple transition.

As you consider the word transition, what comes to your mind? A transition is a moving from one time of certainty to a new time of uncertainty with a period of insecurity in between. The midlife transition is a bridge between early and middle adulthood. Do you know what goes on in a man's mind at this time?

Many men take a hard look at their past. They appraise what has been accomplished during the past ten to twenty years. There is a heightened awareness of their own mortality and this often includes a desire to get more out of the remaining years of life. Some express it this way, "I want to *get* more out of life." Others desire to use the remaining time more wisely.

Part of the midlife transition is coming to grips with our illusions. An illusion is a misleading or deceptive idea. We can be deceived by others and we can deceive ourselves. As a man reappraises his life he often discovers how much has been based on illusions. He is now faced with the task of "de-illusionment." Some handle this much better than others. Putting away illusions is a desirable and normal pattern of adulthood, but not without pain. It can lead to cynicism and estrangement from others, and the man may find it hard to believe in anything. Often Christian men express this change in anger and bitterness toward God. They held to the illusion that if they attempted to lead a godly Christian life, they would be free of some of the difficulties and struggles which others experience.

But not all disillusionment is negative. Reducing illusions creates diverse feelings: from disappointment, joy, relief, bitterness, grief, wonder and freedom. And these also result in different consequences.

Enter the Enemy

For many men, midlife is a time of confronting several enemies. One such enemy is his body. It no longer responds as it used to for it moves more slowly and perhaps even sags. His body doesn't look as good nor does it have the stamina and energy it once did.

The war escalates as he confronts another enemy—work. He may feel trapped with nowhere to go, bored and often in financial bondage. Even men who have a prestigious position feel that there has to be something more fulfilling than this.

A third enemy is his family. Frequently, he feels trapped. If he didn't have financial obligations to his family he could quit his job and live off the land. But tuition for Christian schools, the children's braces, credit card debt, mortgages and car payments are part of the bondage he feels.

God often becomes the fourth enemy. He is viewed as unfair and is blamed for the bind in which the man finds himself. God catches the responsibility for a rotten job, the bodily deterioration and the urges and drives which are creating chaos.

Ask some middle-aged men about their feelings toward their body, work, family and God! Listen to their answers!

As with anything new in one's life, we do not always know how to handle the newness. You may at times hear and see responses in your man which you could call "irrational." They may be in contrast to what the man was like before. But the change may not be that radical. It may be your own inability to handle another person's change that is creating most of your own discomfort.

Often the man's transition is labeled "sick" and this is unfortunate. These changes reflect a normal transition as he works on normal adult tasks which need to be faced. His questioning and modification of life may frighten his wife and friends but it stems from a healthy part of him. He needs to be able to doubt and search at this time. The major question which concerns both his wife and himself is, "What are the answers? What will be the outcome?" It is all right for the man and his family to experience a time of uncertainty at this point for this hesitancy contains the potential for growth.

Dealing with the Baggage

What hinders men is the baggage which they bring with them from their earlier years. Often their bitterness, dependencies, unresolved angers, anxieties and guilt (which have laid about unresolved) interfere with their progress.

If all of the changes which occur at midlife would happen in a very logical, straightforward fashion with a sense of certainty, both the man and his spouse (and friends) would feel better. But false starts and changing one's mind are very common. Why? Simple. There are some confusion and impulsiveness, but also a desire to explore and experiment. How does this affect others? It unsettles those around him who were dependent upon the stability he provided. He appraises and reappraises and each reappraisal is painful for him.

It is not uncommon for a man to want to "go back" to earlier days. This may be an attempt on his part to make up for lacks that existed earlier in his life. Perhaps over the years he was too busy to keep up with relatives, high school or college friends from long ago. Now he may want to look up a former friend or business associate from years ago or become very interested for the first time in attending his high school reunion. Sally Conway says it so well, "This is all a part of the process of looking back over the territory he has covered up to this time in his life before he starts out across a new frontier."[4]

The more radical the change, the more pain he feels—primarily because of the opposition he experiences from those who have an investment in his stability. This can include family, co-workers, church members, his boss, his parents or his colleagues.

Many men go through their inner questioning and change and emerge with more creativity than ever before. They have reviewed life and given it new meaning. Creative abilities and resources emerge and are intensified at this time of life. You see this best described in the life of one of the world's greatest poets, John Milton. He lived in England in the mid-seventeenth century during a time of radical social change. He suffered severe misfortunes in his own personal life including blindness at the age of forty-two. He believed strongly in a just God and was enraged at the injustice which occurred in God's world. In one of his most famous writing endeavors, he allows us a glimpse of his own midlife struggle which is also reflective of so many men:

> Which way shall I fly
> Infinite wrath and infinite despair?
> Which way I fly is hell; myself am hell;
> And in the lowest deep a lower deep,
> Still threat'ning to devour me, opens wide,
> To which the hell I suffer seems a heaven.[5]

What depresses some men is admitting that their misfortunes are a result of their own choices and no one else's. They alone are to blame.

Do you know that some men are so struck, so beaten down, so engaged in a struggle for survival, they cannot listen to nor respond to their inner *call for change?* This denies the man the opportunity to bring new meaning to his life. Any inner flame or desire he had is stifled and extinguished. Some of these men die in their forties or become alcoholics.

There are approximately thirty million men in America between the ages of forty and sixty. All of them go through the midlife transition, but how many of them experience a crisis? A third of them experience the change as a time of turmoil with rapid and dramatic personal and behavioral changes. Why is midlife a time of crisis for some men while others experience a family-balanced adjustment? Can we determine who is crisis-prone? The answer is a definite yes!

The Causes of Crisis

There are seven main theories which have been suggested as the cause of midlife crisis. After all is said and done, each of them has a similar underlying theme.

One theory has been called *The Goal Gap* and is tied to a man's work and career. The main assumption is that a man's personality is primarily determined by his work and career. This is his source of identity or self-esteem. In midlife most men are faced with assessing what they have done in light of their career aspirations and what they had hoped to accomplish. They must also consider what they will be able to do in the time that is left.

The goal gap is probably the most common cause of the male midlife crisis. In our country we have high career expectations but also certain limitations. The higher the education and the more a person knows, the more both the man and other people "expect him to accomplish." But career opportunities are not unlimited and often a man runs into a ceiling as he climbs up the ladder. This produces a career crisis and if it occurs during midlife, it feeds the midlife crisis. There are real and perceived inequities in the working world as both men and women are well aware.

Unfortunately, much of a man's self-worth in our society is based on what he accomplishes in his career. Many men accept the goals of their company or organization as their own without examining them to see if this is truly what they desire. They come to believe that a career is an end rather than a means to an end.

You see, the wider the distance between the man's goals and what he has actually accomplished, the greater the threat. And when a man hits a plateau in his career with little possibility of moving upward, it can be an unsettling experience. How does he react? In various ways!

1. He may simply set aside his goals and withdraw from what he has been pursuing. Some men accomplish this through a careful evaluation of their lives, but others do it through an angry reaction.

2. Some men doggedly continue striving for the goal with increased effort within the same company or organization—or they move on to another.

3. Some men revise their goals and stay in the same career arena.

4. Still others make the switch to another career which gives them a better opportunity to attain their goals.

At this time the man wants to make some type of change. It is helpful if he can share his thoughts and feelings with his wife. But her response can be helpful or detrimental. If the proposed changes appear too threatening and radical, a wife may react negatively, with shock or even ridicule: "You can't be serious!" A man needs the freedom to talk and think through his feelings without his wife reacting negatively every time he brings up the matter.

Another theory concerning the cause of a man's midlife trauma is called *The Dream*. Men have dreams. But many men set aside and neglect the pursuit of their dreams because of family, career and social demands. They repress their dreams and for a while reconcile themselves to this. Often in midlife these dreams emerge once again, forcing the man to confront and deal with them. This may precipitate a crisis.

Just because a man has met his dream, however, does not assure him of avoiding a midlife crisis. Many men who have attained their dream ask, "Was it worth it?" or "Now that I have attained it, where do I go from here?" They are less concerned about where they are going than they are about the cost. They have paid to get there. They now face the size of the bill they paid and how inflated it has become.

Another reason suggested for the midlife crisis is *The Search for Adventure*. Some people believe that men have a fundamental desire for personal growth. And if they see themselves stuck in a rut or stagnating, they will begin to regenerate themselves. Many men see the routines they have carved out for themselves at work and at home as neither stability nor security but a rut! Sameness is not creative nor growth-producing! Thus to bring vitality, adventure, challenge and growth back into their lives, they change their lives radically. It doesn't really matter whether they actually attain some new goals or dreams. The action or quest is really what matters.

Another interesting theory about the midlife crisis is called *Step Aside*. As a man reaches middle age, he discovers that society has different expectations of him than when he was younger. The more challenging and arduous work assignments are given to younger men. Even family and community roles change. The man now faces a time when he has to change to meet these new roles and expectations. He often begins to consider more of what *he* wants out of life than what society expects of him, and he makes some personality and behavioral changes. It almost appears that in middle age a man is being asked to step further and further aside from center stage and this continues until he retires or dies. This stepping aside necessitates finding a new place for oneself and for some it becomes radical.

Another theory involves *The Empty Nest*. Many a man in his fourth or fifth decade faces the children leaving home and the wife returning to school or a profession. His wife and children are no longer that dependent upon him. Established roles are changed and the family no longer revolves so much around him and his moods and activities. They now revolve around things over which he has little or no control or involvement. The empty nest can be as much of a concern to men as it is to women. Male response to these changes can feed a crisis. A man may have feelings of unfinished business with his children. Perhaps he now realizes how much time he *didn't* spend with his son or daughter and would like to catch up. This is a prime time for fathers and children to share their feelings because in many ways the older adolescent and the man at midlife are experiencing similar identity issues.[6]

Another theory which may come as no surprise is called

Vanity and Virility. Inevitable physiological changes happen to all of us at middle age, male and female alike. Men do notice the changes in their bodies and performance, including changes in hairline, skin, body tone, weight and so on. One of the most upsetting changes may involve sexual performance as desire and ability begin to wane. There are sound medical explanations for these changes, but these reasons do not satisfy the man's concern over the threat to his vitality and virility. A major threat has entered his life, and to compensate he may experience radical changes in his personality and behavior. The stage is now set for a midlife crisis.

Finally, *Meeting Mortality* is a seventh theory. Many events occur which cause a man to acknowledge his own mortality. This could involve his own health, the death of his parents or a friend. He may attempt to purchase an insurance policy and the increased rates because of his age and life expectancy come as a shock. It is common for a man to think less in terms of what he has already accomplished, and more in terms of how little time there is left to do anything more. This lack of time can cause a person to reorder his life's priorities.[7]

It has been five years since I have studied and written on the area of midlife. I notice a difference in my own attitude and perspective from the age of forty-four to forty-nine. At times I look at my own age and ask, "How many years are left to me? Will I live to the age of seventy-two as my father did? What about a friend of mine who died two years ago at the age of fifty-three?" I do consider how much time is left and what I want to do with that time. These thoughts have brought about changes in my lifestyle and work. I try to use my time more wisely and choose those activities and work opportunities which I enjoy more.

Is the Cup Half-full—or Half-empty?

As men reorder their priorities, some decide to take advantage of the time that may be left and attempt to live life to the fullest. Yet others appear to resign themselves to the inevitable, withdraw from life and simply give in to their belief that there is little time left.

There are valid arguments for each of the beliefs or theories. There is probably no *one* theory which can sufficiently explain every midlife crisis. But there is always one underlying cause for the midlife crisis, a common thread which is inherent in each theory. *A man's midlife crisis is caused by threats to his identity.* Whether it be the threat of the empty nest, the loss of youth or not meeting one's expectations, identity is involved in all seven theories. Each claims a different source of identity for the middle-aged man and the threat to that identity as the cause for the crisis.

How do some men escape the crisis even though they must face all these factors? By relying upon several sources for their identity rather than one or two, these men can handle the changes of life much better. With multiple resources, they are less vulnerable to loss. They can fall back on other sources for who they are if one or two become shaky. But if their identity is based upon a limited area and that area is threatened, a crisis may occur.

Men make themselves more susceptible to upheaval at midlife by not having developed close male friends nor having learned how to share their feelings with others. Put these three factors together—a limited source for identity (mainly work), no close male friends and not sharing feelings—and you have an excellent basis for a crisis. A man's work may build his identity for a while, but what happens if, instead of leading to riches, it leads to poverty?

Remember these three facts:

- All men experience some type of midlife transition. Not all experience a crisis.
- Many midlife crises can be avoided by changing the cause.
- Men can survive the midlife crisis and move ahead in a positive way.

Who are the men who survive and how do they do it? There are no simple cures, but there are some effective steps which a man can take to resolve the crisis. It is important that both you and your man know what they are. A man needs to:

1. *Recognize* the changes occurring in his life.
2. *Acknowledge* the changes for what they are—threats to his identity.

3. *Consider the consequences.* What is good and what is bad about what is occurring? How should he respond?

4. *Choose to change.* He needs to increase his commitment to change and improve his choice of a change by involving others. This includes sharing his feelings and dreams about his life with someone else.

5. *Integrate the change.* Resolution of the crisis occurs when a man integrates his changed perspective and pattern of behavior into his personality.

When a Wife Works—How Men React

Men do not like the feeling of neglect whether it is real or perceived. Men who have career wives right from the start of their marriage and men whose wives began to work at midlife are no different. They both admit to the same feeling—neglect and abandonment! Men do not want to feel this way but it is difficult for them to discuss the discrepancy between what they *want* to feel and what they are actually feeling.

One wife said to me, "We both agreed that it would be good for me to work. We enjoy the extra income and the benefits, but I don't think Jerry was prepared for the changes. Sometimes I return home later than he does and he has always expected a nice dinner. But that takes time! And I'm tired on the weekend. He may want to take off and play, but I have to catch up with some necessities as well as get some rest. And if I have to go out of town for even one night, I can predict his reaction down to the minute! He gets quiet when I tell him and the next couple of days he withdraws, gets grumpy and finally, in an angry voice, asks if the trip is necessary. He already knows the answer, but he asks anyway. I don't like what's happening. I end up feeling like I'm his mother in some way, and darn it, I'm not!"

Often a wife returns to work when the children are in older adolescence or are leaving the home. For most couples, this happens right at midlife. There are two possible results from the wife's new role: A man may once again have to face his dependency needs and the feelings of neglect he had when he was growing up. He may resist the changes necessary which make him remain stuck in his midlife transition. Or, he may work through some of the myths that he has held about himself and his father as the sole breadwinner and become a free-growing individual.

Let's take a closer look at what transpires when the wife goes back to work. When a wife enters the work force with a new career, the roles in the home have to be altered. He leaves for work in the morning and so does she! She has new experiences, meets interesting people and confronts new ideas. He may do the same or he may not. Her world is a bit foreign to him. She likes to discuss this new world and his needs are no longer primary.

It isn't just a discussion of *his* career that lends excitement to the household anymore, but *hers* as well. He may feel he has lost his position as "the center of the universe." His wife is alive, vibrant and excited about her new career and challenges, just when he is starting to reevaluate, level off and even slow down in his own career. Career is old for him, but new for her. What about competition between the two of them? What if she succeeds faster and to a greater degree than he? What if he is boxed in and the sky is the limit for her?

For some families, it is not only the children who are being launched but the wife as well. And he's stuck. He may be threatened by the new men whom she is meeting in the business world as well. A wife's self-esteem and influence may increase with her new position and this too upsets some of the balance of the relationship. She may experience personal growth and he may meet with personal stagnation. His beliefs about his own worth, value, self-esteem and identity may be challenged at this point in life.

A wife's entrance into the work force may be perceived by a husband in many ways. Some feel betrayed, others abandoned; some feel like failures and others are open and curious to see how this will all turn out. And they respond to these changes in different ways.

Some men experience an increase of anger and even rage. They threaten and are angry either subtly or in an explosive manner. Why? This is their attempt to maintain the balance the way it was before. Other men become sad or even evidence a passive-manipulative response. Some do show curiosity and encouragement because this new experience holds the potential for growth.

Avoidance is a classic response at this point. The man plunges into his own work more and more and accentuates what he does. Often he plunges into many tasks at home in an effort to point out what his wife is no longer doing and to show that he can carry both roles if necessary.

At this time of life a man needs to be encouraged to face his feelings and share them in a safe context. There are usually some irrational fears plaguing the man, such as losing his wife if she becomes too self-sufficient. He may feel she does not need him anymore nor want him because of all the other men around her. This fear is naturally not easy for men to talk about.

A man may feel shame at not being able to discuss his feelings, sort them out, handle or accept them. The shame may be accompanied by anger and both need to be expressed. The anger may also be tied to his sense of loss.

For many men it is easier to become angry than to face the loss, sadness and tears. When a man is angry, it is often helpful to respond with, "I can hear your anger and I accept it. I wonder if there is another feeling though, such as a sense of loss or sadness. If there is, I would be willing to hear about that as well."

This is a good time for a man to talk about his own father as he faced midlife. How did he age and handle adjustments? What didn't he talk about that his son wished he had discussed? Unfortunately my father died when I was a young man. He was fifty when I was born and seventy-two when he was killed in an automobile accident driving home from work. I wish I could have asked him some of these questions. The time spent in this type of closeness is as valuable as the answer.

Midlife brings changes for everyone! Samuel Osherson describes it well:

> While husbands at midlife often see themselves as different from their wives and children, the irony is that they truly share a common bond with their families. Each is facing the task of redefining himself or herself in the world: The wife struggles

with exploring new options, her feelings of insecurity in venturing beyond the confines of the mother role balanced by her curiosity about new possibilities that await her. The children are launched into college, confronting choice and possibility, identity, career, and intimacy questions. And in truth, those are some of the same questions that the father confronts anew at midlife: What balance of work and intimacy do I want? What are the central values and purposes that will fill this new stage of my life? How do I maintain my self-confidence and self-esteem through this time of change? The father himself, with or without the help of his family, may work to make himself more isolated or resistive. Yet the crucial task in most rearranging families is to see that all members really are going through a shared experience of self-exploration and change.[8]

How a Woman Can Respond to a Man's Midlife Transition

It may come as a shock to you, but women appear to be more concerned than men about the man's midlife crisis and what to do about it! Women speak up more about it and perhaps that is because women seem to be more inclined to deal openly with emotional and psychological concerns than men. Why are women more concerned? Because they are the ones who have to deal with both the changes and the consequences of the behavior of the middle-aged man. This is true in the area of both marriage and work. A woman is affected by the changes in her husband, in the man she is dating or those in her business world. And the man in midlife crisis *needs* someone close to him to help him navigate as he seeks to find a solution. Those who don't have someone to assist them have difficulty finding a resolution. And a man needs someone to do more than just "be available." A woman can do specific things to help a man resolve his midlife crisis, things which relate to the steps he needs to take:

A woman needs to help a man *see* himself.

A woman needs to help a man *understand* himself.

Helping the Man See Himself

The woman in a man's life probably sees him with greater perception than anyone else. She has a unique vantage point from which to observe his behavior. A woman is able to note the entire picture of what is occurring and has the best opportunity to hold the mirror which can reflect to the man the changes in his perception and behavior. But sensitivity and skill are so vital. As one man reflected, "Oh, my wife tried all right. But the way she tried drove me deeper into my problem and even away from her. She was so certain that she knew what my problems were and what the answers were. She saw herself as an expert and kept quoting some blasted book to me! She came across as a judge over everything I did or said. She may have been concerned about me, but it didn't come across that way. I felt she was more concerned about how the changes were going to mess up her life than about me."

Another man reflected a different story: "My wife was a tremendous help. She could see what was happening to me and shared what she saw, but in such a way that I could handle it. What she said made sense and she never judged me or accused me. She described to me what she saw happening and how she felt about it. She wasn't a know-it-all either. I can remember her saying that she didn't have all the answers either. And what really gave me support and encouragement was her telling me she was actually willing to help me experiment and find some answers. Can you imagine that! She wanted to work this out with me and I didn't end up feeling alone with all the burden. This made it easier for me to look at what I was experiencing."

If you share with a man in such a way that he feels evaluated and controlled (and with an absence of caring), he will probably be defensive and reject what you say even though you may be correct in your observations. If, however, you share your reflections about a man in a descriptive, spontaneous manner with empathy and willingness to experiment with him for solutions, he will be more willing to hear your observations.

Some men in crisis make rash statements about giving up a job, selling the house, cashing in the life insurance policy, traveling for a year or living in a cabin in the woods. These statements threaten other people and may seem like options.

Overreaction on the part of a wife at this time is not the answer, but helping the man think through the consequences of his decisions and considering other possibilities can make a difference. Saying, "You're out of your mind," or "You do that and I'll divorce you and take every cent you've got" are not the best responses! Listening to a man and helping him clarify and identify what he is thinking often helps him realize how unrealistic his ideas are. Encourage him to discuss them with you. Make a list of the negatives and positives and discuss with him the realities of the consequences of this radical change. But be open to suggesting modifications and alternatives to his plans so he does not feel trapped even more. There are occasions when a man can make sufficient changes in actions he is already doing.

There are five things a woman can do to help a man see himself:

1. Any information you share with a man about his behavior should be descriptive rather than an evaluation of what he is doing. Any suggestions such as, "You should . . .", Why don't you . . .", "If it were me, I would . . ." are probably going to be rejected. Just make observations and be sure to employ the next suggestion.

2. Be specific in what you say, not general. Suppose someone were to say to you, "You're different. You've really changed." And you ask, "In what way am I different? How have I changed?" And the person replies, "Well, you're just different than you were. I see a change in you." You would probably end up confused and would reject the idea that you had changed. General statements do not help. We need specifics.

But suppose someone said, "You don't seem to be as alert or tuned in as you used to be," or "Your reaction to my suggestion seemed overly strong compared to your usual reaction." You would know what the person sees that is different in you. In talking with your man, there are vital phrases to use to make sure you understand one another. When you talk with him, from time to time ask, "What do you understand me to be saying to you?" You need to do this or you may assume erroneously that he understands what you are saying. It is also helpful to reflect back to him, "This is what I think I hear you saying . . . Is that accurate?"

3. Don't make your comments at random. Watch your timing. Proverbs says timing is critical. Ask yourself the questions, "Is he ready to hear it? Can he relate to it? Is what I say really reliable?" If at all possible wait for him to ask your

opinion or for your observations about his behavior. If he doesn't, ask, "Could I make an observation about what just happened?" or "I'm not sure about what just happened, but here is the way I see it. I'd like to know how you feel about it."

4. Avoid giving solutions. Instead, help him in the process of problem-solving. Your purpose in making an observation about a man's behavior should not be to control him, but to help him solve the problem. And you are doing this *with* him. Don't try to teach or judge him.

5. Be sure you don't give him sympathy. Try empathy instead. If a man senses genuine concern and respect, he can hear what is being said. He needs to sense that his needs are being taken into consideration.

Never say to him, "I know what your problem is. You're just having a midlife crisis." Labeling a man is the best way to push him away. Men do not like to be labeled by an "expert." And this kind of statement implies that the woman knows more about what is occurring than he does. This doesn't sit well with middle-aged men.

Helping the Man Understand Himself

How is this accomplished? Following the previous five points helps. If he senses your concern, he will be open to your exploring with him the causes for this desire to change which is gripping him. A major reason for onset and continuation of a midlife crisis is the inability and unwillingness of a man to be introspective, to take a close, intimate look at himself. He should be encouraged to doubt, to question and to be concerned about himself.

If a woman is overly dependent upon her husband and relies upon him for her strength and stability, she is going to be terribly threatened by his changes. And she may respond in such a way as to prolong his crisis. How? By not encouraging him to face and fully experience what is occurring inside him. Don't discourage him from being introspective.

Be patient during this time of adjustment since you may discover your husband is quite changeable. He vacillates greatly in what he wants and what pleases him so you will find it difficult to meet his needs. This is an unsettled, frustrating time for you, but that is because it is an unsettled, frustrating time for him! Be resilient!

Every woman needs to ask herself, "Am I in some way contributing to his crisis?" Some women overly reinforce what a man does and achieves in his career. If a man's identity is built upon one area and a wife supports this singular identity, it may make it more difficult for him to find an alternative identity. Any concern expressed for your man should be for his sake and not for yours. Some have difficulty with this because they are more afraid of the consequences for themselves than for the man. And he will sense this. *He* needs to deal with *his* crisis so *he* can be happy rather than having to make both of you happy. Mutual satisfaction *can* occur as a natural outgrowth of the man's resolution of his midlife change.

Help Him Change Himself

As he talks about change, even though it may appear radical, do not overreact. Having someone listen to some of his thoughts and feelings will assist him in settling the issues. Many of the changes men make at this time are quite sound and solid.

If you can accept the fact that some change is necessary as a means for growth and reinforce his change as much as you can, you will be able to give him the support he needs. In midlife, some change is going to occur and a woman can fight it and prolong it, or face and accept it—and thus become a positive influence.[9]

Christians and non-Christians alike experience the change. It is to be hoped that a Christian will see a different meaning in the midlife changes. For some the changes are threatening. But for us Christians changes present an opportunity to apply our faith and develop toward maturity. It is not just a burn-out time of life but a time of harvest and new beginning, a time of enrichment and stability. A Christian has the opportunity to make this a time of creative growth and positive change.

Change that is threatening to a nonbeliever can be an opportunity for a Christian to exercise his faith. Even these changes are expressions of God's love. Through God's strength the midlife experience can make life richer and more in line with his will. Neither a man nor a woman has to fear the middle passage of life. It can be a time of enrichment as we face the meaning and reality of the various changes. Stephen Shapiro summed up this midlife struggle so well when he said, ". . . The only values worth living for after midlife are those which shine in the face of death."[10]

One last thought: Identity is a major issue for *both* men and women. And even though it is helpful to have a multitude of sources for our identity there is really only one solid basis for identity—and it can't be earned. In fact, that's the good news. We don't have to knock ourselves out attempting to capture it. Our identity as believers is a gift from God. He is the one who gives us our identity because of what he has done for us through the gift of his Son Jesus Christ! We are declared to be somebody and adequate because of how God sees us! It's something to think about.

Note: This chapter in concluded but for many of you reading this book, the topic is not closed. You may need to do some additional reading. Here are three resources which can help:

Seasons of a Marriage by Norman Wright (Regal Books).

The 40 to 60-Year-Old Male by Michael McGill (Simon and Schuster). Check your public library for this outstanding book as it is unfortunately out of print.

You and Your Husband's Midlife Crisis by Sally Conway (David C. Cook).

10

Men Under Stress—It Affects You, Too!

What can I do if the man in my life is under considerable stress? A foolish question? Not at all. It's a real concern in our time in history. We all live with and encounter stressful situations. But stress seems to have more deadly effects on men than on women.

Twice as many men die from combined diseases of the heart as do women.

Pneumonia and influenza cause about three times as many male deaths as female.

Accidents and adverse drug effects kill three times more males than females.

Men commit suicide at a rate of three to one compared to women. There are thirty percent more male deaths than female from cancer (which can be stress related).[1]

Men seem susceptible to stress in other ways as well. More males die as fetuses during their mother's pregnancies, at birth and as newborns. Men live shorter lives than women. The average age now is seventy-eight for women and seventy for men. It appears that from birth to old age, men are more prone to dying before their time than women. And men exhibit more stress-related problems than women such as hypertension, arteriosclerosis, heart attack and heart failure.

The causes of stress in both men and women are many. Stress can occur from anything that annoys, threatens, prods, excites, scares, worries, hurries, angers, frustrates, challenges, criticizes you or threatens your self-esteem. Anything, whether it is unpleasant or pleasant, that arouses a man's adrenalin system and mobilizes his body to either fight it or run from it, and then does not let up and give him time to recover, can have some severe effects.[2]

Life is full of the potential for stress. We all face it. With the increase of information concerning stress during the past decade, a person would have to be blind not to be aware of its existence. Sources of stress cannot always be eliminated and so the change must come in our response to them. The men in your life, whether a husband, business associate, son or male friend, can be a potential source of pressure and stress in your own life! Men are aware that stress affects their bodies and their behavior. But they need to be convinced that the damage is happening *now!*

I've talked to many men who say they know that in time stress will have a negative effect on their life but they emphasize "in time." A hint of denial exists. Many men have to feel the symptoms first before admitting there is a problem. As one forty-year-old man said, "Look, I haven't had any heart problems, or ulcers or high blood pressure. I'm really all right. When my body begins to cry out to me, then I'll listen." The problem with this approach is that changes occur slowly and quietly. The man's body may be crying out with a silent scream, but his ears do not hear it. Today's stress is the cause of tomorrow's personal difficulties. Today's stress, unfortunately, affects other people today, not tomorrow!

Who takes the brunt of the stress in a man's life? Everyone—his family, friends and mainly himself, but especially his heart! The heart is the main target of destruction for much of the harmful stress a person experiences.

Most individuals today live in both a competitive and demanding situation. For many men, this starts at a very early age and keeps them striving to get ahead. Many live their lives in a constant state of hurry or even emergency. When this occurs, unconsciously we become dependent upon an overproduction of adrenalin to accomplish our goals. This strategy works, but the cost is much higher than we imagine. The cardiovascular system experiences more and more wear and tear and we don't even realize what is happening to us until the symptoms emerge. You have undoubtedly seen the person who has tolerance for frustration and is highly driven and always in a hurry. Label that person a candidate for heart disease. He (or she) is a high risk.

Do you know the four major areas of male stress? Georgia Witkin-Lanoil, from her decade of working with men under stress, has clearly identified four major focus areas.

Body Concerns

You wouldn't know it to look at some men, but for the majority, their body image *was* important. As boys, height, weight and athletic ability were primary. As young men, sexual ability was important. In middle age, stamina is a major concern. After that, health becomes the major issue. Men are strong, but which sex lives the longest? Men are aware of that discrepancy.

Career Concerns

Listen to the question put to a little boy, "What do you want to be when you grow up?" And the question is repeated again and again as he grows. Notice the question is "What . . ." It isn't *who* he wants to be or *how* he wants to be but *what!* At an early age a man can become preoccupied with his occupation. His identity and self-worth are all wrapped up in the same package. The messages he receives from earliest days are: provide, produce, do well, earn lots of money, make choices and above all be in control. But life doesn't always turn out as we expect or predict. When his career and work are unpredictable, a man's achievement is stifled, expectations are unrealistic and control is out of reach. The result? Stress grows.

Family Concerns

A man has to adjust to the shift from being a son for twenty years to the role of husband and then father. And the majority jump into these roles with little anticipation or preparation. Most men put in more time preparing to obtain their driver's license than they do to getting married or becoming a father. Men in their twenties assume many roles with many demands and each role carries the unpredictable label. For those who experience divorce and then remarriage, the stresses are multiplied.

Personal Concerns

Most men do not realize how common personal concerns are. Why? Because too few men share these concerns as well as their inner feelings. Men tend to increase and escalate the intensity of their pressure points. They do this in two major ways—by not sharing their innermost feelings and by the lack of close male friends. They go it "alone" and show the world "I am a man." It appears that setting a good example of strength is more important than resolving inner concerns. But having a confidant is actually better than relying upon inner self-confidence. A lack of communication showing the bond with another person is a vital factor in the increase of stress and its effects.[3]

Men and women have similar stress but also experience many pressures that are dissimilar. And among those they have in common, there are even many differences. Unfortunately, both sexes have little understanding of each other's particular stress. Men often view women as "complainers." And many women see men's upsets as minimal in comparison to premenstrual symptoms, pregnancy, childbirth and menopause. Women do have a physical makeup in the reproductive system which both creates stress and is vulnerable to it. But men have a higher *fatality* risk from their stress symptoms. The basic question is not who has it worse, but how can I understand the other individual to make it better?

Let's consider a few of the stresses we all face and note the unique differences between the coping mechanisms of men and women.

The Clock Is Ticking

The passage of time with its uncertainties and low factor of predictability can be stressful for both men and women. But within this there appears to be a more personal meaning for each. For women it seems their biological clock runs "too fast." Men, however, feel their achievement clock is moving "too slow." By a certain age they would like to have achieved specific salaries, positions and types of recognition. Men's decade birthdays are important measures of success. What have you achieved by the time you are fifty? Men tend to have bigger celebrations on their fortieth and fiftieth birthdays than women. In some ways they enjoy drawing attention to these dates.

Does a woman? Not too many have the desire to call attention to their fortieth or fiftieth birthdays! Men like the notoriety at these times if they have been successful. If they haven't, at their party they may laugh and act like they are having a good time. But inwardly they may be despairing.

Writing *this* volume has become more for me than an academic experience of just writing another book. Throughout the time of research and discussion, I have done a lot of thinking and feeling about myself. I try to apply what I am writing and several times I have mentioned to my wife Joyce what I have learned about myself as I write each chapter. In some ways, I fit the patterns described and in others I do not. As I unearthed more evidence concerning the way men respond to their decade birthdays, I reflected on my own thoughts and feelings prior to starting work on this treatise.

Joyce and I will turn fifty in 1987. I tended to ignore my fortieth birthday but I have considered more and more how to celebrate this next milestone in a special way. Why? Perhaps it's a way of accepting, facing and welcoming the half-century mark. This also involves recognizing all that God has done for me during times of delight, enjoyment, fun, unique experiences, pain, sorrow and loss. It is a time of thanking him for bringing a fullness and meaning to life no matter what has occurred. It is also a way of saying I am ready for whatever he has in the future—and it is all right not to know what to expect. That is risky! The unknown and unpredictable become the known and predictable because of who is in charge of my life and life itself.

Facing some of these midlife birthdays is a way of admitting that half or two-thirds of your life has been completed. And more and more you ask the question, "Where does my life go now and what do I want to experience?"

Both men and women have a *desire to achieve*. But the stress encountered along the way varies for each. Men are taught to be more openly competitive. Whatever you do, "win, win, win." Whether it be with a group, a team or an individual activity, winning is the best. Men do believe that hard work pays off but it also creates compulsive competitors. A man competes with others on the job, for a promotion, with the memory of his father—and men even compete with themselves!

In the past, women have been taught to be closet competitors. They have been more likely to hide their competitive efforts and feelings than men.

What is the source of stress for men? Where there is low job satisfaction, shame and guilt arise. And the more they dislike their work, the more stress they feel when they mention to others what they do for a living. For them work becomes a trap![4]

Is Sex Stressful?

It certainly can be! A man's sex stress is performance anxiety. Since performance is so vital to the male's image of masculinity, it is no surprise to find sex as a measure of what a man can accomplish.

If a man can't perform, it is obvious! Whereas women can fake some responses, a man cannot fake an orgasm, an erection or arousal. He certainly cannot hide a "failure." And if his ability in sex wanes as he ages and his wife's does not, he feels pressure. When he experiences his first encounter with impotency (and all men experience this from time to time because of stress) it can be shattering. He now develops anticipatory anxiety to add to his performance anxiety—and the more he tries, the less happens.

If you know anything about stress, you're probably asking, "Is all stress negative? Isn't there a positive factor in stress?" No and yes. "No," all stress is not negative and "yes," there is a positive side to stress.

Good stress involves a brief feeling of exhilaration. Bad stress brings about long-term psychological and physical erosion. So much of the stress I see in people who seek counseling has to do with the feeling of being out of control. A man forced to retire before he decides to leave, being fired before he could quit, a son injured with no identifiable prognosis, a spouse disabled, a parent with a sudden stroke are all examples of control being taken out of our hands.

Stress Can Be Good—or Bad

There are four factors which distinguish between good and bad stress. One is your *sense of choice*. If you *choose* something which carries a sense of pressure, it can feel more like a stimulating experience than stress. Some men have an adrenalin addiction. They thrive on the stimulation of a challenge. They choose the pressure. Unfortunately, there are some who choose too much pressure and the stimulation becomes excessive and stressful without them knowing what is happening to them.

But when we have pressure put upon us with no control, we experience it as stress.

Secondly, *control* is a major factor. Real and perceived stress increases as one feels his amount of control diminishing. There are major and minor events which occur in life over which we have absolutely no control. And some of these events come swooping into one's life like an alien invader. Men who have an excessive need for control experience greater stress when they do not have control. In many cases the proportion of control needed by a man is in direct relation to the amount of insecurity hidden behind that controlling veneer.

Sources of Stress

I'm not sure that we are totally aware of all the sources of stress in our lives. How a man responds to stress will vary. Some men have learned to accept the unpredictability of life and they are much better able to handle life's surprises. Others are thrown by life itself. Some men become stressed by changes in simple routines, by going into new social situations, by the fear of failure and even by their children.

One of the biggest sources of stress occurs when men feel a situation is beyond their control. And it can be a very simple situation!

- Men are stressed when they are forced to be in the passenger seat rather than at the wheel of an automobile.
- Men are stressed when they must wait for a table at a restaurant, or in line for a movie, and they frequently choose to forgo the meal or movie to regain their sense of choice.
- Men become infuriated by road construction and exasperated at "stupid" drivers who distract or detain them.
- Men dread funerals and psychotherapy, and sometimes equate the two as depressing reminders of life's uncertainties.
- Men postpone dental appointments and other procedures that require them to put themselves in other's hands.
- Men are terrified of illness or injury that may interfere with their ability to be in charge of their daily lives.
- Men prefer requests to demands, and free choice to requests—and they will demonstrate this by saying "no" to suggestions for things that they might actually have enjoyed.[5]

A third stress-related factor is the *ability to anticipate consequences*. When demands and outcomes are unpredictable, it is more difficult for some to make the necessary adjustments in life which are predictable. These individuals are bored and stagnating. Others live on the edge of unexpected anticipation constantly and their bodies are wired.[6] But the fourth factor which helps to bring stability and lessen stress even when the first three are lacking is a *person's attitude*—an attitude which has captured the stability of a biblical perspective on life's difficult situations.

Each person, man or woman, has the ability and the freedom to choose his or her response to life's difficulties and problems. We could say, "This situation is intolerable. This is totally upsetting. This is the last thing I needed. Why now and why me?"

The other way one can respond to the same difficult situation or problem is, "This isn't what I wanted or expected, but it is here and I have to face it. It's going to be a difficult time. How can I make the best of it and learn through this? How can I grow through this? How can God be glorified through this?"

One of your concerns about the man in your life may be his inability to admit to stress. Many men simply ignore the symptoms of stress or they may admit to the symptoms, but believe age is the cause, not stress. In the past I, too, have been guilty of this. Some of the most common symptoms women see in husbands, sons and their own fathers are: headaches, insomnia, allergies, teeth grinding and jaw clenching, nausea, indigestion, heartburn, backaches and stiff necks. Men may admit to these but age is often considered the villain.

Symptoms of Stress

Men seem to add to their symptom list as they age. Note the following chart based upon a survey of men.[7]

	Ages			
Symptoms	18–29	30–39	40–49	50+
High Blood Pressure				X
Muscle Aches			X	X
Gastritis/Ulcers			X	X
Heartburn		X	X	X
Headache	X	X	X	X

Be sure you encourage the men around you to have complete and thorough physicals with a doctor who is knowledgeable about stress and its specific symptoms.

Heart attack! The very mention of it strikes a note of fear into the hearts of most men. Why? Because it is so common and men are more prone to die of a heart attack than women. A man's susceptibility is not due just to his physiology but also to his psychology. The highly achievement-oriented, competitive man who has success in his career is also very prone to experience a heart attack.

I'm sure you have heard of the Type A personality. This individual deeply affects the lives of others in a stressful manner. His stress feeds the stress of others. Type A behavior is a continuous struggle to achieve more and more, or to participate in more and more activities in less and less time. The Type A man charges ahead, often in the face of either real or imagined opposition from others. He is dominated by an inner hidden insecurity about his status and self-esteem—or he is dominated by super aggressiveness, or both. It is easy for him to be overbearing and dominating. This man, whether he be twenty or fifty, has such a sense of time urgency that we say "he has the hurry-up sickness!"

The Type A man is competitive. There is nothing wrong with a balanced sense of competition, but the Type A person is out of balance. His sense of competition is intense. Motivation comes from the thrill of victory and he hates defeat. He competes at work, play, in the family and, of course, with himself. It is difficult to relax around this man.

Impatience is a common characteristic. Any delays or interruptions create irritation. But it's all right for him to interrupt other people to show them better and faster ways of doing things. He finishes sentences for people and even though he knows better, he punches the elevator button several times to speed it up. He has refined numerous ways to glance at his watch or a clock to note the time.

Overscheduling of activities for himself is common and he will attempt to do the same to others. He has polyphasic behavior and thinking which means he attempts to do several things at the same time. You can see him drinking coffee, looking at a magazine, talking on the telephone and beckoning to another person to come into his office. Extreme demands are placed upon his thinking ability, energy source and even digestion. He feels the only way to get ahead is to function in this way. Why waste time?

Other characteristics include a low tolerance for frustration and a high level of aggression. He cannot relax without feeling guilty and he often suffers from low self-esteem which leads to free-floating hostility.

There is a major penalty for choosing to live life in this way. What is it? The Type A man is five times more likely to have a heart attack than the Type B person. The Type A person is responsible for wrecked lives and careers for himself and others. There are three arterial diseases believed to be initiated or provoked by Type A behavior: migraines, high blood pressure and coronary heart disease.[8]

How many of these creatures are there? Depending upon the studies you read and whether the population is urban or rural, it is estimated that between 50–70 percent of our population fall into the Type A category in some degree.

Can life in the fast lane be slowed down? Yes! I have seen both men and women change. What can you do to help the man in your life who may be this way? Read! There are suggestions to follow in my book, *How to Have a Creative Crisis*. Perhaps in following the guidelines there, you will be able to get your man's attention so eventually he will read *Adrenalin and Stress* by Archibald Hart (Word) and *Treating Type A Behavior and Your Heart* by Meyer Friedman and Diane Ulmer (Knopf).

How to Recognize Stress in a Man

Of all the indicators of stress, behavioral signs are the most helpful because you can recognize them and they are usually repetitive. A man may not be aware of these and he needs someone else to identify them early! The following is the result of a Male Stress Survey conducted among hundreds of women. These are the early behavioral signs of stress in men as observed by women.

1. A man becomes verbally abusive or critical of his wife or children. This was reported as number one.

2. Withdrawing and appearing silent or preoccupied was the second most frequently reported indicator of stress.

3. Men often tend to overeat and gain weight during times of stress.

4. They also tend to drink more alcohol during stress periods.

5. Unusual fatigue is a stress signal for some men.

6. Some men work off their stress by plunging even more deeply into their work or activities. They exhibit agitated activity.

7. For those who smoke, the smoking rate increases because it is used as an antidote to stress. And during stress it is difficult for people to cut back.

8. Some men experience physical symptoms such as teeth-grinding, tapping the fingers, swinging the feet or engaging in minor compulsive behaviors when faced with stresses of all types.

9. There is an excessive tendency to fall asleep when faced with stresses of all types.

10. Selective deafness is quite common. The man tunes you out even though you think he hears you.

11. Reckless driving and the tendency to take chances reflect stress. The driving pattern can create stress for the other family members.

12. Television addiction can be used as a distractor. The man may not even watch the television while it is on, it is just a distractor.

13. Watch for facial gestures such as tics, eye blinking, excessive swallowing and so on.

Some of the other characteristics which may occur are increased spending, compulsive sex or, more commonly, a loss of sexual interest.[9]

What did you notice about the previous list? Did you see how many of these are actually stress distractors and how many can lead to additional stresses? None of these behaviors should be ignored for they affect the body, the job and the family.

Psychological Early Warning Signs

There are several psychological indicators of stress. Some of these may be characteristics of a man for other reasons, but they are frequently accurate signs that need to be heeded. Any one of these six "D's," as one author has described them, can indicate the beginning of stress. More than one could indicate moderate to high stress. I have seen some men with all six warning signs!

Defensiveness is a way of denying that anything is wrong. It can be a way of trying to fool others—or the man can actually believe his own rationalizations. This often reflects the unrealistic expectation that a man should always act like a man: "Be strong and don't admit problems."

Depression is a reflection of loss and anger. And it is the loss of control which bothers so many men.

Disorganization has an effect upon concentration and thus a man may forget, repeat himself or not make good decisions. This is one of the key signs for myself that I am encountering stress. I tend to forget and become a bit disorganized even though I have my two calendars and keep my lists!

Defiance is a form of attempting to regain control. It gives a man a chance to fight back and often there is no real reason for responding in this manner.

Dependency reflects regression which happens to men under stress. It would be nice to be taken care of but most men are not about to admit this to someone else.

Decision-making difficulties are common. Even minor decisions may be difficult to make at this time. Feelings of lack of control or choice can block a man from being decisive.[10]

Remember that men differ in how much stress they can handle and how they respond to stress. Their tolerance levels vary and each man experiences stress with a different intensity. Some of a man's symptoms have been learned from role models and from his experiences as he was growing up.

How can you help a man under stress? You could suggest to him some of the stress reduction techniques recommended in several books (see *Stress/Unstress; Treating Type A Behavior and Your Heart* and *When I Relax I Feel Guilty* by Tim Hansel). These include exercise, meditation, relaxation techniques, evaluation of life's goals and time management. A man needs to be encouraged to become involved in developing healthy responses to the imposed stresses of life and to discover how he creates his own inner stress. Don't be surprised by your man's reaction when you offer wise counsel and positive suggestions. Too many men do not listen to the advice of their wives but ironically will take the same suggestion from someone else.

Don't give up, but be loving and persistent. A man who learns to exercise, laugh and cry, and share his burdens with others is developing an excellent antidote for stress. Above all encourage him to talk by providing a safe environment in which to share. These principles can be used with a father, son, brother, friend or husband.

You can help a man with his stress by following some of the principles we use in talking with people who are experiencing a crisis. Stress is often the first step to developing a full-fledged state of crisis. Thus by helping a man with stress, many a crisis can be avoided. Here are some guidelines:

1. One of the first principles to remember is *not* to become an authority on the other person. Don't say, "I know what your problem is . . ." or, "You're under stress and this is the reason why. If you'll only listen to me . . . ." You may know more than the man does, but your presentation will determine whether he accepts or rejects your help.

2. Men under stress need someone who cares. Those who survive a crisis are those who have a close friend who sticks with them during their time of difficulty. A person who cares sees the stress from the other person's perspective. You may be frightened or panicked by what is happening to your man, but sharing that anxiety does not comfort him. Concern is acceptable and is often reflected in your tone of voice and nonverbal expressions. Comments like, "I would like to understand what you are going through" or, "Is this the first time you've experienced this or has it happened before?" are helpful.

3. Encourage the man to talk about what is occurring and, if possible, how he feels about it. Remember that the latter may be a limited possibility if feelings are not a part of his vocabulary. As he talks he can listen to himself and the process of talking out loud may help him eventually resolve the problem. Try statements like, "I'd like to hear it from your perspective" or, "Tell me a little more about that rough board meeting."

4. Practice James 1:19—"Be a ready listener"—and Proverbs 18:13, "He who answers a matter before he hears all the facts, to him it is folly and shame." Listen actively but remember that listening means you are not thinking about what you are going to say as soon as he stops talking. It is all right to reflect back what you thought he was saying.

"If I understand you right, you're . . ."

"Is this correct? You feel as if . . ."

"If I caught what you're saying, it's . . ."

5. Do not make or allow the man to become dependent upon you. As I work with individuals under stress, they often want to be rescued. They need to learn to help themselves. Otherwise, their leaning upon us can create new stress for them as it lessens their feeling of being in control.

6. Years ago I had the opportunity to study under Dr. William Glasser who wrote *Reality Therapy*. His simple style

of counseling works extremely well with people undergoing stress. One of his main theses was to develop a plan. He would ask his clients, "Well, what's your plan? Everyone has to have a plan." And that is exactly what you can do to help the son, father, friend or husband who is under stress. "Have you thought of a plan yet?" "What are the different plans or alternatives you've thought of?" "What do you plan to do?"

As plans or alternatives are suggested, help him look at various alternatives and the possible consequences. In dealing with stress there are numerous options such as going for a physical, working to change your perspective on a problem, altering expectations, giving yourself permission to be out of control, learning relaxation techniques and so on. Help your man refine his focus on what he can do and what he will be unable to do.

7. In crisis counseling, we ask for a commitment. You could do the same here, and there are two strong reasons for doing so. It clarifies the fact that it is the man's responsibility to follow through and second, if he does so, it will help to elevate his self-esteem. Do not assume that discussing it one time will resolve the problem. You may have to go through the process again to refine and clarify. If the person is a Christian, ask if he would like you to pray with him at that time. Let him know that you will be praying for him and it would help you if he could give you indications of what he would like you to pray about in his life.

In responding in this way you not only function as a support to the man under stress; you also can be assured that you are not contributing to his stress level.

11

The Arena

"My husband is having an affair!" She spit the words out as she sat there in my office. Her angry look told me that her feelings had been building for some time.

"I just figured it out the other day," she continued. "He's been having this affair for the past several years. And it's not with a woman. It's with his job! That's his wife, his mistress! That's all he seems to live for. It's work, work, work! It gets the priorities, I get the leftovers. I get his worn-out carcass at night. Work gets his mind, his attention, his emotions even when he's at home. I can tell by that preoccupied look on his face that he's still involved with his job even when I'm talking with him."

She stopped for a minute and then went on, "And I'm not the only wife who feels this way. We've discussed this problem in our Bible study class and most of us are struggling with our husband's preoccupation with his work. Why can't husbands approach work like normal persons? Why do they get so involved? Why does it seem to consume their life and have so much meaning for them? Are there any answers? And more important, are there any solutions? I don't want the next thirty-five years of our life to be like this!"

Important questions. Common questions that deserve an answer. Few men are free from the compulsion to work. The majority of men need to work. Often a man has a passionate and even painful love/hate affair with his job. Into his work he puts his competitive drives, his need to win, his aggression and his desperate search for his own identity.

Most men feel their work is more important than their wife's work. If a man believes his work defines who he is, then

171

it's important that his wife's work be perceived as secondary to his. If your job requires that he give something up, don't be surprised if you meet with some resistance. (There are many exceptions to this type of man, however.)

Too many men are defined by their work—and so is their status. The more important the job, the more it may pay; the higher the status, the greater the feeling of self-worth it confers. Outside recognition on the job can boost the man's estimation of himself. Employment is important. If the significant man in your life were unemployed, how would you feel? Think about it. If you're married and you were out with your husband and met someone, how would you feel if your husband's response to the question, "Well, what do you do?" was, "Oh, I'm unemployed." Most wives are not against their husband's work. Rather, they are opposed to the lack of balance and meaning which the work creates.

The Career Trap

Many men today are in a career trap. They may have trapped themselves into working so much because of their or their wives' economic desires. And then the pleasures of work become outweighed by the pain of overinvolvement.

They live with the words "work-work-work" screaming inside them and they allow the words to become a command. Eventually they end up selling their lives, their wives, their children, their enjoyment for the position of a slave. Unfortunately, these are men who live with the motto, "I am my job." How sad such an existence is. Some of these men do wake up to their distorted value system, but it often takes a heart attack or the loss of family to do it. For a wife who is concerned about this tendency, creating a positive crisis may bring about a change (see my *How to Have a Creative Crisis*).

Please don't assume that all men like their jobs. The majority do not and wish they could do something else. Often they don't know what it would be, however. In the classic book by Studs Terkel, *Working,* only a handful of those interviewed liked their profession. This is sad and it creates stress for the man and those around him.

Women take more of a pragmatic approach to work. They see employment as a means to an end, but a man views employment as the end. Most everything in a man's world is connected to his work. If you were to ask a woman who she is, she would probably respond with a number of terms describing her relationship with the world and people around her. Not so with a man. He will probably reply with a list of what he does and what he owns. This could include his house, car, clubs and associations, titles, duties, responsibilities and hobbies. A man's work is the way he can maintain all of these items.

Where did the infatuation with work begin? Probably when the man was a young boy. Most boys learn to value themselves in terms of achievements, successes and victories. How does it happen? He receives applause and rewards from his parents and friends as a boy when he runs faster, speaks better, reads earlier than others, wins a game, gets high grades or does anything that shows he is a "winner." From an early age men learn to respond to "You did a great job!" as well as, "It'd be great if you did that well too." When you're a winner, you're treated in a special way. Losing, failing or being incompetent brings rejection and disapproval. As the boy grows he internalizes these parental attitudes and messages until it is his own inner voice that says nice things to him when he succeeds—or will insult him when he doesn't.

If he doesn't achieve, he then draws on this reservoir of abuse which can flood his lack of achievement. And what is unfortunate for many men, even when they do succeed, these little voices break through and say, "But you could have done even better" or "So and so did a better job than you did."

All of this means that his emotions and moods are tied into his successes and failures. Elation comes from succeeding, and shame and embarrassment come from failing. You may not realize it since he has also learned to hide these feelings. He wants to protect his image and present a façade of one who is successful and in control.

Lifestyle and work—which one determines the other for men? Some men work to live and others live to work. There are a few men whose work fits their lifestyle but for most, their lifestyle revolves around their job. My father worked hard to scrape together a living. He worked long hours and often six days a week. His daily routine when he arrived home was very predictable as was his use of time on the weekends. Survival was very important to him as it is for anyone who came through the Great Depression.

Even though many men are married to their work, they are also married to a woman. And in today's world, a wife and children will not be content to exist with an absentee husband and father.

Today work has taken on much more meaning for many of us. It is what we do, where we do it and who we are! Ask a number of men what their work means to them. You will hear responses like the following:

"It's who I am."

"It's my meal ticket."

"It's a way to get to the top."

"It's my way of not having to live like my parents did."

"It's a calling from God."

"It's my collegium. It's where I can butt heads with others and come out on top."

"This is where my creativity shines. I can express myself through my job. I realize not everyone is that fortunate, but I am."

Ken Druck describes the potential of work very well when he says, "Our work can be either a source of enormous personal fulfillment and liberation or a burial ground for some of our most disturbing fears and secrets. Work should be the stage on which many of our greatest performances in life are given and our most satisfying moments are lived. Men who love their work are often sustained by it through dry spells, loss of loved ones, sudden changes, or crisis in other areas of their lives."[1]

Why Men Work

There are numerous reasons why men work. A man works because God has called him to work. A person cannot really move through life adequately without working for just simple survival needs. Men work to express who they are. It's a way of saying to the world, "Here is what I do! This is what I have accomplished." A man steps back and looks at his achievement with a sense of satisfaction. He becomes less of a nameless face in the crowd through his accomplishments. It's a way to distinguish oneself.

Men work to have a purpose for living. For some, work justifies living. Work provides meaning and significance. But a balance is needed since so many men who retire at age sixty-five become depressed and even suicidal. Without work there is no meaning in life left for them.

Many men work to feel "a part of" something greater than themselves. Work provides them with relationships with others. A man feels good in providing for his family at home and also gets satisfaction through his teamwork contribution at work or in society. He discovers that he really does fit and can contribute. Men and women have a need to contribute. God has called us to make a contribution to society and to others.

Work brings satisfaction. It doesn't matter whether you work with your mind or hands, body or thoughts, there is something satisfying about being able to express your abilities. Skills are refined by work and even if a man is in a profession in which he doesn't always see the fruit of his labor, he can say, "I feel good just knowing that I worked today." I've heard men say, "Boy, I worked hard today and I don't know what I accomplished. But it feels good just to be tired like this. It tells me I worked."

Work is an opportunity for men to make an impact and difference in their world. One man said to me, "When I die, I want my absence to be noticed for years to come. I want to change my community, my city and yes, even the world in some way. You ask me why I work. That's why. I'm putting my brand on the world around me and it's going to stay. I want people to miss me."

A man works to improve his station in life. This can involve money to purchase those items which we feel we need for the good life. Our work brings recognition and a new status and respect.

Men work to enable them to move to a better neighborhood or to drive a sharper car which others will notice. They work so their children will not have to go without as they did.

There is this drive to improve which is good as long as it stays under our control and we don't allow it to control us.

These are just some of the reasons, but before you read on, I would like you to do something. Take a piece of paper and if you are married or have a close male friend, please do the following. Write down five reasons why you think this man works. Then ask him, "Have you ever identified the five major reasons why you work? I'd be interested in knowing what they are. I've written down five of my own for you and I'd like to see if I really know your motivation. When you write yours down, I'd like to hear them and then share my ideas with you." When he begins sharing, take it one step further. Ask him where he thinks these reasons were learned. Then ask him, "Ten years from now and then twenty years from now, why do you think you will be working? Will it be because of the same reasons or different ones?" I think you will have a very interesting conversation.

Hiding in Your Work?

Men use work for other reasons also. Have you ever considered how men use work as a hiding place? A man's work may not enrich his life as he hoped it would, but there are other benefits which can be derived from work.

Work is a great place for a man to hide his feelings. The feelings which create a state of discomfort in a man can be buried and hidden by plunging into work.

Work can also become a hiding place for the fear of failure. How? Some men ward off their concern over failing by staying busy. If a man senses failure or feels that he isn't doing as much as others, he can accelerate his time at work. It's a great way to hide our inner sense of inadequacy. This type of behavior, however, sets a precedent that others may come to expect and the man soon finds himself on a treadmill to nowhere.

Work is often used as an excuse not to live life more fully in other ways. What better way to avoid intimacy than by working unusually long hours! After all, when a man works that much, how can you expect him to have time and energy and interest in people, relationships and family events?

Work also becomes the hiding place for the man who feels inadequate. Work enables him to be a man. This equation leads a man to use his work as a proving ground. And the more insecure a man is about himself, the harder he works. Compulsive work patterns are often the result of inner, driving insecurities.

Have you ever heard a man say, "Of course I love my family and they ought to know it! Just look how hard I work for them!" Bringing home the paycheck is the only expression of love that some men know. The love expressed through responsibility is usually indicative of a man who does not know how to express his love in other ways. For such men showing it is better than expressing it verbally.[2]

You may feel that the greatest competition you have to face with your man is his work. That may be true, especially if work is the source of his identity. What can you do? Listen to him talk about the meaning, purpose and frustrations of his work. If at all possible, go with him a day or so and observe what he does in his work to gain a better perspective. Discover some books or literature concerning his field so you can better discuss his vocation with him. If work and identity are intertwined, suggest that he might want to consider the option of other sources for his identity. A statement like, "You know, many men use their work for their identity and self-esteem and that's one way. There are other options though. If you'd like to know about them sometime, let me know." Don't say anything else until he follows up on your offer. You may be surprised. Many men want out of that work trap, but no one has offered them an alternative. You may be the catalyst for change.

Note: A book to suggest for your man to read would be *Do I Have to Be Me?* by Lloyd Ahlem (Regal Books). Unfortunately, this book is out of print, but the author's two chapters on adequacy are excellent. Check with your church library for a copy to borrow. I would also suggest the book *The Sensation of Being Somebody* by Maurice Wagner (Zondervan). One last resource which I would encourage every business person to read is *Living on the Ragged Edge* by Chuck Swindoll (Word). This book raises several important issues about work and some practical and biblical solutions.

12

Men Who Never Grow Up!

Yes, there are some men who never grow up! Throughout their entire lifetime, in one way or another, they respond as a child. And many of them have no desire to change. Whether they change or not is their responsibility, but it is important that the women in their lives not fall into the trap of becoming their mothers!

How Should You Respond?

When you work with, have a relationship with or are married to a child-man, at times you think you're going crazy. You begin to doubt your own sanity and ability! You become frustrated and angry.

When I talk about a child-man, I'm not talking about men in general. All of us have some childlike tendencies. There is a little child in each of us and that's all right. What I am talking about is the man who does not behave like a man in his relationships with other adults. Listen to the following conversation. Perhaps you have felt this way or know someone who has.

Confused and angry, Nancy sat in my office. She tried to explain her dilemma:

"When I married Fred, I thought I'd married a grown man. He seemed to be responsible and was really charming when we went out together, but since we got married I feel as though I'm married to a child. In so many ways he's never grown up. And I don't want to be his mother! I don't know what to do with him anymore! I've tried so many different responses and my mind is running wild with so many questions. I've

178

heard that men are still little boys in some way for most of their lives, but this is ridiculous. I want to love him, not mother him."

When she paused, I interjected a question: "Can you share with me what is going on inside your mind? What are you thinking and feeling?"

"I'm confused," she continued, "but at least I've made a list of some of the questions and thoughts I've had over the past few days. Here are some of them: Why do I feel like I've done something wrong or feel guilty when he's angry or cruel to me? Why does he always have to have things his way? And I mean always! Why do I vacillate so much? I say no and then give in because of his persuasiveness. Why can't I depend on his word? Why do I end up feeling like yelling at him as though he's an irresponsible child? Why can't he love me the way I would like? Why do I often feel like his mother? Why is he so irresponsible, but then I cover for him and make excuses? And what really irritates me is why I end up sinking down in his level.

"I thought falling in love with a man would bring happiness, but what I have is misery. Why was I so dumb that I didn't notice the way he was when we were going together? Why can't he say 'I'm sorry' when he messes up? Why does he ignore me so much when we go out? He pays attention to others and is really charming, but not with me. Why is he so faithful to his male friends, but doesn't even help me with little things I ask him to do? The only time he shows concern is when I get on him and complain and gripe about his indifference and then for a day or so he responds. But then he lapses back into the same pattern of ignoring me."

The Peter Pan Syndrome

There are men like this who have symptoms such as these to one degree or another. Let's consider ten basic symptoms of the man Dr. Dan Kiley has given the label of "Peter Pan." Taken from the story of Peter Pan, this is the man who has never grown up. Dr. Kiley states that every woman has known one, loved one, married one, left one or survived one, but no woman can resist one! That's quite a statement. What about you? Do you fit in any of those five categories? Let's look at this child-man. What is he like?

He is *undependable* though quite charming and witty at the beginning of any type of relationship. In time, however, especially when you need him the most, he tends to become invisible when he grows bored or when responsibilities are placed upon him.

He is *rebellious*. When you make a request, he interprets it as a demand. His ways of rebelling are numerous and creative. Two of his passive responses (which can be extremely irritating) are procrastination and forgetfulness. Some have called this emotional blackmail.

He is *helpless* in terms of the number of problems with which he cannot cope. Women are drawn into assisting him with problems that seem to overwhelm him but which he should be able to handle.

He is *narcissistic* or in love with himself. Who does he think about? Not others! *He* comes first and because he cannot empathize, he cannot comprehend why his wife gets upset. And worse, he won't try to see it from her perspective.

He tries to elicit *pity* from his wife. Pouting and sulking are common. He attempts to appeal to the mothering instincts of the women in his life. He is a great complainer but makes little effort to change his unhappy circumstances.

Guilt is a part of his life, especially in his relationship with his parents. Usually he is resentful toward Mom but longs for a close relationship with his dad.

In so many ways, this man is *dependent*. He will not reciprocate love, concern or care unless his wife gets on his case—and even then his response will vanish quickly.

Words like *manipulator, con artist* and *dishonest* appear on your lips when this man comes to mind.

Often you are drawn to the "little boy" in him, but when you reach out in an attempt to get close, he withdraws. He is very *secretive*.[1]

There is a sense of *emotional paralysis* because the man's emotions are stunted. He tends to express a different emotion from the one he is experiencing. Anger is expressed as rage. He may tell you he loves you but somehow forgets to express it.

One reason for his procrastination is the belief, "Why invest any energy? It will only end up in more failure."

This type of man is often socially impotent. Even though he is involved with others and inwardly suffers from acute loneliness, he cannot make friends. Unable to face the fact that the inadequacies in his relationships lie within himself, he may attempt to buy friends. He engages in magical thinking such as "If I don't think about the problems, they will go away." Avoidance abounds.[2]

What are you feeling right now? If you are like many women you are probably experiencing strong feelings of frustration as you recall interacting with such men in the past, or the frustration of being married to such a man right now! "Peter Pan" men can be helped to change but it is a slow process. Since they resist therapy and the admission of problems, many will never change. These men must come to the place of admitting the problem, discovering that their way of responding is ineffective and be willing to change. The women in their lives must consider two vital factors: 1) Be sure you do not fall into the trap of mothering (which may mean changing your way of responding); and 2) be sure you don't have the need to mother a grown man! Unfortunately some women do!

What to Do and What Not to Do

Do not mother men! Most men do not want to be mothered. When he tricks you into that response, you help him remain a child.

Don't let denial become a part of your life. Denial is saying, "This is not happening to me. He is not this way." How does denial express itself? You excuse his behavior with alibis, ignore his selfishness, dismiss the feeling that something is wrong or keep reminding yourself how much you care for this man even though he treats you atrociously. You inconvenience yourself, pick up his clutter for him, write him notes so he won't forget and try to hide those items he should have remembered. Denial is dangerous since it may spread to other areas in your life as well. Allowing a man to continue to act as a child does not help him—nor does it really show love toward him.

Denial can hide your own pain from you and make you vulnerable to the approaches of another man.

Overprotection is a typical mothering device. "Why, he can't possibly make it without my help and support," you say. Wrong. This type of responding robs both of you of your individuality. Soon you begin to take on the man's problems as your own and feel the weight and responsibility of them. Be sure you don't have a "need to be needed" in this way. This is not a healthy pattern of life. Overprotection manifests itself in various ways.

If you are possessive of this man, there is a mutual problem. Some women say, "I just can't make it without him; I cannot stand being alone." If this is the case, you will probably put time demands on the man. Asking for reassurance of his love, you will experience jealousy when he enjoys time with others. You will not think of enjoying yourself unless he is with you. This is not what the scripture means when it says of married individuals, "The two shall become one."

One of the great responses of all time (it has been with us for thousands of years) is complaining. You've had enough and your man is going to change or else. Your intentions may be good, but does complaining eliminate the problem or perpetuate it? Your frustration level can build to the point that the complaints are no longer given in private but in front of others. And I think we all know what happens when we publicly embarrass another person. This builds guilt and that does not motivate. Instead, it builds resentment and the man may tend to forget even more.

Complaints cover a wide range including:

"You don't share your feelings with me."

"You don't love me."

"You don't cooperate with me."

"You don't help me or take an interest in the children."

"You're not interested in spiritual matters."

"You smoke (eat, drink, sleep) too much."

Pulling the Strings?

Complaining soon moves into another response which elevates the woman into the position of judge. You become an expert on this man. And if a man goes along with your judgments and changes for a time, you are now in the role of a puppeteer pulling the strings and—once again—mothering. You become the expert by telling the man how he feels, what his behavior means to him, what he is really thinking. When telling (not asking) him to do things, you give the instructions in such a way a kindergarten child could do it. What does this type of response say about you as a woman? It's something to consider. (By the way, for further amplification of this chapter you may want to read *The Peter Pan Syndrome* and *The Wendy Dilemma,* both by Dr. Dan Kiley.)

Some women take the sacrificial lamb approach. They become martyrs which involves self-blame. This both reflects low self-esteem and creates it. "What did I do to make him behave this way?" "I'm just too sensitive." "I'm sorry for crying." "I'm worried about saying the wrong thing." These are common responses. What you are trying to do is find out what you are doing wrong so you can fix yourself (you think this will fix the relationship). You protect the man by blaming yourself so you don't have to blame him. You do his work for him, admit you're wrong when you are not, experience self-pity and so on. But such activity does not bring about change, build a relationship or fit the pattern of biblical submissiveness—nor does it glorify God. (You may find it helpful to read the outstanding book for women, *Finding Inner Security* by Jan Congo [Regal] for assistance in this area.)

When the above approaches don't work, there is always punishment. "Make the beast pay for the way he is and how he has treated me" is the angry cry. There are many ways to punish a man. You can scream at him, spend too much money, eat too much and put on weight (if he hates overweight women), give him dirty looks especially in public, bring up past mistakes, badger him about one of his defects, deny him sex or put him down in public. All of these reflect a form of mothering since they include verbal and nonverbal spanking and denial of privileges.

A final way of responding is just giving up and becoming depressed. Totally down on yourself, you've run out of ideas and become immobilized. This approach along with all the previous ones does not work. What then?

Respond as an adult, not as a mother. And be sure you ask yourself these questions first.

If I am attracted to a man like this, or married to one, does that say anything about my own needs?

Is my self-image intact and built upon the truth of scripture? Do I need this kind of man to fill an empty place in my life?

Before I attempt to respond differently, what are my expectations and desires? Do I want to change me or him or both? What if he does not change no matter what I do? Can I still function and not be frustrated? Responding in a nonmothering way is a way of fulfilling the scripture admonitions of "encouraging, edifying and building up one another and admonishing one another to good works."

It would take more room than we have here to list all the possible ways of responding in an adult, positive manner, but here are a number of suggestions to stimulate your thinking. The purpose of these suggestions is to help you with your own personal growth and to encourage the man in your life to become a caring, mature person. If your man tends to overreact and one way or another attempts to get you to excuse his behavior or failings or appease his guilt—be sure you *don't* let him out of his responsibility by saying something like, "I'm sure you did the best you were able to do" or "Others were at fault and you were the victim of circumstances." Do not support any of his rationalizations.

What can you *do*? You could ask him how it feels to make a mistake. You can ask him what he could have done differently. What did he learn from this and what will be done differently the next time? You could offer some alternatives. "We all become angry and that is quite normal." Watch out for the anger which will be directed your way when you don't feel sorry for him. It will come. Be sure you don't take responsibility for his problem or his anger.

A man like this needs to experience the consequences of his irresponsible behavior.

If your man has the habit of forgetting important dates and appointments—including your anniversary or birthday—

be sure you don't drop subtle hints, complain to others about him or try to shame him.

You can place the dates in bright bold letters on the calendar both of you use. Tell him just before the important date that it's about to occur.

Let him know how important remembering dates is to you and why it is important. Ask him how he is going to develop his plan to remember the dates the next time. If he says, "I just forget. I need you to remind me," don't buy this line. I'm sure there are some dates he does remember which are important to him. Say, "No, I am not going to remind you, but I will work with you to develop the plan you are going to follow in order to remember."

A woman wants the man in her life to be dependable. This has a direct bearing on trust and security for most people. It's unfortunate that some of you will have to be involved in assisting a man to mature, but it can be done! I've talked to many women who are upset over having to pick up after their husbands. Some men were extremely sloppy and the major excuse is, "I forgot." That is no reason.

Several wives have shared with me that they made the decision not to pick up after their husbands any more. They were tired of their husbands' failure to help with chores around the house, forgetting to pick up items at the store, missing commitments to the children and so on. One wife said that her husband seemed to go around the house in a fog. He left his clothes all over and even some of his work reports. For eight years she followed along behind him, straightening and picking up and putting things in order. One day the revolution came. She didn't pick up, but just piled his items in stacks or even in the corner of a room. When he began to notice and ask for what he needed, she replied, "Oh, I think it's in that stack over there. I just don't know. I guess you'll need to look for it." In time his behavior changed.

Another wife was tired of her husband's complaints about his parents and the problems with them. For years she listened to his complaining, but saw no action. One day she sat down with him and together they made a list of all the alternatives he had for responding to his parents and the different approaches. From that point on, whenever he began to gripe, she said,

"Honey, I've heard this many times before. We did come up with a list of alternatives. Please refer to that." She refused to participate in his griping and in time he would go back to the list and find a better way to respond.

If your man is more attentive and sensitive to others *don't*—

—Expect him to attempt things he isn't good at.

—Compare him to other men who do help or point out that he helps others and not you.

What can you do with this man? You can expect him to complete the tasks you ask him to do. Make plans to do some tasks together and be sure you reinforce in a positive way what he does accomplish. Ask him what kind of a time frame he needs for the task and how you should respond, if for some reason it isn't getting done.

Perhaps you're getting the idea at this point that you are not going to live his life for him, nor are you going to mother him, nor are you going to participate with him and reinforce his irresponsibility.[3] Again, for more practical suggestions, see *The Peter Pan Syndrome* by Dr. Dan Kiley.

There is another type of man-woman relationship which needs to be addressed. In 1986, a new book appeared on the scene titled *Men Who Hate Women and the Women Who Love Them* by Dr. Susan Forward. The response to this book (which made it hit the best seller charts) must say something about the extent of dissatisfaction many women feel with the relationships they experience with some men. In this book, the author begins by describing the inadequate basis upon which many couples start their relationship and marriage. They are blinded by their expectations and unrealistic romantic love all entwined together. Some of the chapter titles are self-explanatory: "How He Gains Control—Weapons"; "Where He Gains Control—Arenas"; "What Keeps Women Hooked"; "How Men Learn to Hate Women"; and "How Women Learn to Love Women-haters."

The first part of the book describes the problem and why it develops. The man in focus here is one who is genuinely responsible and competent when he responds to society in general. His destructive behavior is focused upon the women in his life and his weapons are his words and moods. Usually he does not physically abuse the woman but wears her down through psychological battering. A woman is, in time, demoralized by this pattern. A man like this is a misogynist, which means woman-hater, and the relationship which continues is a misogynistic one.

Such relationships often begin with a high degree of romance which can include whirlwind courtships and romantic blinders. But in time the relationship begins to deteriorate. At times the man is wonderful and at others just the opposite. One of the themes which emerges in the woman's mind is the thought, *If he can be so wonderful, then I must be doing something wrong to make him respond the way he does.* As the honeymoon ends, the man begins to attack his partner, using implied warnings, verbal criticism and actual threats. He tends to control the bedroom, finances, social contacts, time with the family and how to respond to the children. The wife gets the message that she is supposed to be perfect as well as read his mind.

The second part of this insightful book talks about feelings, preparing for change, healing the past, taking charge of anger, setting limits with one's partner and getting professional help. In a very practical manner, the author describes the relationship between thoughts and feelings. Feelings are an important source of information about ourselves. But most of us are not aware that our feelings are usually a direct result of thoughts. Before there can be a feeling, there is often a thought. We all talk to ourselves or carry on inner conversations with ourselves. This is perfectly normal. Negative, demeaning thinking will lead to negative depressive feelings. Thus it is important to learn to distinguish thoughts from feelings.

Whenever you have a feeling, try to identify the thought behind it and you may be amazed. The author presents a helpful list of questions to assist you in identifying your feelings and the questions focus on such feelings as sadness, fear, hopelessness, confusion, guilt, frustration, a sense of feeling trapped, and so on. As I read through these questions, it appeared it might even be more helpful if you would evaluate yourself on a scale of 0–10 for each one with a 0 meaning "I don't feel this way at all" and a 10 meaning "I feel this way with great intensity!"

Identifying your feelings and the thoughts behind them will enable you to then change your behavior and your reactions. In a very helpful manner the author describes the process of listing and identifying the thoughts which generate the emotions.

Dr. Forward then proceeds to discuss the behaviors which are created from the thoughts and feelings. Again it might be helpful to respond to these questions not only as the author has suggested, but on the basis of a scale of 0–10. The behaviors listed in this extensive and insightful list include apologizing, accepting blame, walking on eggs, crying, figuring out how to obtain your partner's approval, giving up your own activities and opinions, excusing your partner's behavior, letting yourself go physically and many more. Identifying these behaviors will enable the reader to realize that there have been distressing thoughts and feelings in operation.

Following the personal evaluation, Dr. Forward then suggests evaluating the behavior of the man in your life with a series of twenty-three important questions. Answering ten or more of these with a "yes" answer would indicate that you are involved in a misogynistic relationship. And once again, for additional clarification, I would suggest the 0–10 evaluation to help identify the behaviors in an even more specific manner.

The questions range from controlling you, criticizing you, intimidating you, frightening you, withdrawing love and approval, blaming you, confusing you, accusing you of being too sensitive and many more. It is quite apparent that even though this is not a book written from a Christian perspective the behaviors identified are definitely not biblical behaviors.

The purpose of these exercises is to assist the reader to change the quality of her life by changing her own behavior. Of course this will feel awkward and uncomfortable but that will be minimal when compared with the results that are possible. Too often people believe that just accepting the status quo is the easiest and least threatening. But the cost has to be considered as the relationship often becomes worse!

The remainder of this book gives some helpful guidelines on how to change your response to men such as this.

It is vital to realize that you will need to change your own behavior rather than making direct attempts to change your partner's. But this carries the possibility of bringing about a change in a relationship. The only person who needs to learn to do things differently would be yourself. And Dr. Forward again makes practical suggestions with believable illustrations from case studies. Some of the suggestions include becoming an observer of your reactions to your partner's attacks; realizing that the choice to behave as you do is your own; identifying and writing down the labels your partner has used against you and change the way you see your partner.

There are many additional techniques and responses which have been described in many other books but are here applied specifically to this particular problem. They include changing your thoughts, identifying new assertive statements, rehearsal of these statements, considering the consequences to name just a few. If you have such a relationship, I would recommend reading Dr. Forward's book. It is a secular book and you will need to evaluate some suggestions in the light of the Scriptures.

Ideally we would hope that a Christian man would not respond in the manner described by Dr. Forward. But unfortunately there are men and women alike who have taken their own personality disorders and superimposed them upon their faith instead of allowing the presence of Jesus Christ to become the change agent to remake them into new, loving, secure persons.

I wouldn't want you to assume that most men are like the two problems identified in this chapter. Some could have a few of these characteristics but it is important that we do not go about labeling men. If the behavior is apparent and blatant, however, then the man probably fits into one of these categories.

Women who are involved with such men and maintain relationships have usually cooperated with them in some way to encourage and perpetuate the behavior. *But they are not responsible for the man being this way!* It is vital to pray for change in your life to break your patterns of response and to pray for the man. Then take positive action. Perhaps you are thinking, *But I've tried and nothing has worked!* or *This doesn't sound much like being submissive.* We are not called to be submissive to reinforce and perpetuate damaging, immature non-Christian responses. And perhaps you have tried, but now there are new ways to respond which perhaps you have not tried.

As you make the changes in your life, remember that you as a believer are not a crippled, powerless person. You are a new creation who has been adopted into God's family. Ask him to accompany you on this journey of change. Remember that your first step is changing your beliefs, thoughts, attitudes and behaviors. There is more possibility that the man in your life will then change. But even if he doesn't, he will not be as effective in his responses since you are now in control of your own life.

13

Sex—What Else Do They Think About?

"Is that all they think about? Good grief! There's more to life than sex. I have to watch what I say, the way I walk, what I wear or he gets that look in his eye. And why can't he be as charming and attentive on the days that he's not thinking about sex as the times he is feeling sexual? And he wakes up that way in the morning. Does he dream about it all night? I have to be careful about the way I turn over in bed or he thinks I'm giving him an invitation."

For the third time that week, I heard this concern expressed in my office by three different wives. But I also heard the following concern as well.

"I'm not sure what's wrong with John. He hasn't approached me sexually for five months. I've tried to get his attention but he doesn't seem interested. I'm beginning to think something is wrong with me. In fact, I've even thought he has another woman but he tells me he loves me, desires me and is not interested in anyone else. He says he's just tired or has too much on his mind. Could that be true? Do men get that way after just three years of marriage?"

A good question.

Men and Sex

What *are* men like sexually? Are they either always looking for sex or totally uninterested? What do you think? Let's see what you believe about men and sex. As you read over the following sentences, decide whether you agree or disagree

191

with the statements. (You may want to ask the man in your life to respond to them also. Ask the people at your work, church or social group to discuss these statements and watch the fun begin!)

1. Men are by nature "women watchers." Women are not usually "men watchers."

2. When a man looks at an attractive woman, he is thinking about sex with her.

3. Men do not usually worry about their sexual performance.

4. Men are more easily sexually aroused than women.

5. The most important sexual organ is the brain.

6. A man can remain sexually active into his seventies and eighties.

7. About half of the male babies are born with an erection.

8. Sex has a different meaning to a man than to a woman.

9. Sex is a way that men prove their manhood.

10. Men tend to use sex to prove that they love a woman.

11. Men are very open in their discussions with other men about sex.

12. A man worries about the size of his penis.

13. Men have a greater sex drive than women.

14. The Book of Genesis affirms our sexuality and the Song of Solomon celebrates it.

We all have our own set of beliefs and feelings about sex. No two individuals think about it or experience it in the same way. We are all sexual, but men are extremely sexual and they think about it more than women. Even Christian men think about it more. Both men and women look at a person of the opposite sex with appreciation for the way that person looks. But often a woman's sense of appreciation is more romantic and a man's look is sexual. Men do look at a woman's curves in a sexual way.

Sexual thoughts flit in and out of a man's mind all day long. Men think about, dream about and daydream about sex far more than you probably ever realized. Even though men slow down in their thoughts about sex when they're in their forties and fifties, they still think about it several times a day. Men tend to dream about sex at least three times as often as women, and their dreams rarely involve their own wives. Women tend to dream about men they know.

The daydreams of men are rich, varied and detailed. Fantasies can create sex that is never disappointing and all types of sexual experiences. This creates problems because very few women can compete with a man's fantasies and often men are disappointed with their real sexual experiences. This is not usually the fault of the woman for very few could ever attain the level of performance and ecstasy that a man dreams about.

You may think that men have few or no apprehensions about sex. False! Men are concerned about their performance, partly because they equate so much of their maleness or manhood with their sexual ability. They want to be sure that they can have an erection, maintain it, satisfy the woman and be certain to have an orgasm.

Achieve-Achieve-Achieve

The performance trap which men create overflows into the sexual arena as well as most other aspects of life. The three "A's" of manhood are Achieve, Achieve and Achieve. Tasks, goals and achievement come by work and men are achievement machines. For many men the performance ethic is the only way to do things. They are uncomfortable with times and situations that are unstructured and spontaneous. This same orientation is brought to sex. If a man does take time to create a romantic atmosphere with ample conversation, it is a necessary step in order to bring about sex. This is tragic since every moment a couple spends together can be fulfilling. Because of their goal orientation, it is often difficult for men to focus on what is happening in the present. And when the sexual act is concluded, rather than finding it enjoyable, men tend to move on to another goal.

Impotence

The greatest sexual fear men have is bound up in one word—impotence. This is the inability to either achieve or maintain an erection. Erections are a normal part of male life. Many male babies are born with an erection. Men have four or five erections a night and often wake up with an erection. This early morning erection is a healthy sign as it indicates that a man is still capable of functioning. The male hormone, testosterone, becomes depleted during the day and is replenished during sleep. It peaks around 5 A.M. and is as much as 40 percent higher than the night before. Men are more capable of sex in the morning but this time is often difficult for a woman because the lovemaking has not been preceded by a time of loving communication. Thus his early-morning erection has nothing to do with thinking about sex. Sometimes it merely means he has a full bladder! Many wives believe that every such erection means he wants sex and many men upon waking immediately think, "Oh, arousal! I must want sex! Let's have sex!" That may not be the case.

The Mark of a Man

Let's consider some facts about men and sex. Men desire sex for a number of reasons. This could include physical release, giving or receiving comfort or affection, love, proving one's popularity, masculinity or sexual ability, and expressing tenderness or hostility. Many men use sex to prove their manhood. As I listen to some of the conversations in the athletic club locker room, I often hear men describing their newest "conquest." Some even mention how many times they had intercourse during the night with their new partner or how many partners they had during the week. Consciously or subconsciously the man is looking for some spoken or unspoken admiration from the others. He hopes they are thinking, *What a man!*

Whether men realize it or not, they do want something more in a relationship than sex. They do want closeness and intimacy, but they do not know how to ask for it or admit to it. The equating of masculinity with sexual frequency leads to emptiness and potential erosion of masculine feelings about oneself. Why? Because a man may come to believe that he should have a greater sexual interest than he has and should perform more frequently, longer and enjoy it more. And if the woman desires sex more frequently than he, he really begins to wonder about himself.

Men do not have the sexual endurance of women. Nor do they have the long-term capability for enjoyment that women have. Today, women are much more insistent on achieving sexual pleasure and satisfaction than in the past. This pressure is seen as a threat to a number of men and may affect their performance.

Most men are capable of expressing love and affection through the sexual experience. But what they need to learn is the giving of love and affection in nonsexual ways. One of the most common complaints that I (and countless other marriage therapists) have heard from wives is, "I wish that he could understand that each time I kiss him or hug him or caress him when I walk by him in the house is *not* an invitation to the bedroom. I even hesitate giving these little responses because we seem to end up in an argument. Why can't he understand? I don't even respond now when he comes up and kisses or holds me. I just know that he's got sex on his mind. If we could have a lot of nonsexual contact I would respond much more and he would really be surprised and delighted!"

A man often interprets his wife's sexual response as a signal of how she feels about him in general. In reality, how often a wife responds or what she agrees to do sexually with him may have little or no bearing on her feelings toward him.

A Substitute for Sharing

Sex is used differently by men and women in a love relationship. Many women view sharing as being close and men view being close as something sexual. Women view sex as one way of being close and too many men view it as the *only* way to be close. For women, tenderness, touching, talking and sex go together. For some men, sex is sufficient, especially if they do not know how to relate in other forms of intimacy.

Men substitute sex for sharing. Sex is an expression of emotion and also substitutes for emotion. As one woman expressed her feelings about sex with her husband, "To me being close means sharing and talking. He thinks being close is having sex. Maybe that's the difference in the way we love. When he's upset or mad or insecure, he wants sex. I guess it reassures him. But I wish he would talk about the feelings. When I get home from work and I'm wound up with a lot of baggage, I want to talk about it. When he comes home that way, he doesn't want to talk, he wants sex. When I'm sad, what I need is a shoulder to cry on and someone to hear me out. When he's sad, he wants to be seduced out of his feelings."[1]

One husband said, "Sex means many things to me. Sometimes I want sex with my wife because I feel romantic and want to be loving and close. Other times I just want the release or diversion. I don't need to talk all the time about it. I wish she could understand that."

Too many men believe that sex can substitute for all the other types of communication in a relationship. Sex is the vehicle to take care of sharing their personal and private selves. It is as though a husband says to his wife, "You ought to know I love you because I make love to you." For women sex is only one means of intimacy out of many and not always the best one. For many men, sex is the only expression of intimacy.

Men tend to compress the meaning of intimacy into the sex act and when they don't have that outlet, they can become frustrated and upset. Why? Because they're cut off from the only source of closeness they know. Men are interested in closeness and intimacy but they have different ways of defining and expressing it. Here again is an area where men and women need to talk, listen, understand the other person's view of sex and in some way learn to speak the other person's language.

Men hesitate to talk with their wives about sex because of their fear of making fools of themselves. Since they are supposed to be the strong, tough ones, they're afraid to make themselves vulnerable. They're supposed to be the sex whose feelings shouldn't get hurt. But men can be vulnerable.

Why should we be surprised that men don't really open up and talk in depth about sex? It is a very private area and it means running a risk. They don't really take risks in other areas, do they? Men are as evasive in disclosing themselves sexually as they are emotionally. Research has indicated that less than twenty percent of the men discuss their favorite forms of sex play, their former sex partners or their sexual fantasies, even with their wives. Men are sexual but not really sensual. Sexual relief is important to a man but what really makes him uncomfortable is nongoal-directed holding and caressing. Thus he approaches sex in a mechanical manner. Sex becomes work rather than play. The end result rather than the process is important. Sex is an act rather than being close. This ignores the fact that a man's sexual response is also an expression of who he is. It is directly tied to his feelings and desires and is also a reflection of the quality of the marital relationship.[2]

More and more men today realize that the greater emotional involvement they have with their wives, the more intense their physical satisfaction. I feel it is important for a wife to share with her husband her feelings about sex and help him to talk about his sexual feelings and what would make it more satisfying for him. All of us can find the sexual part of us enhanced by talking and even reading some of the excellent sex instruction books aloud to one another!

Proof by Performance

Younger men especially tend to prove themselves through their sexual performance but as a man grows older and matures he wants greater intimacy. The intense sexual drive and view of physical affection he had as an adolescent begins to change. As he matures he is able to tell the difference between his need for emotional reassurance and nurturing and his need for sex. Communication does become more important for some men. If your husband approaches you with a hug and a kiss and you wonder what he wants, ask! Find out if he wants a pat, kiss, caress, five minutes of fondling or sexual intercourse. You may be surprised!

Earlier I mentioned that a major fear of men is impotence. Men do worry about their erections. They need foreplay just as women do. They cannot always perform on command. Atmosphere is important to them as well. There are times when a man cannot achieve an erection at all even though he feels aroused and loving. That can be a normal response. If it continues time and time again, it is an indication of some difficulty. As men grow older, their erections may not be as firm and they may take longer to occur. All men will experience a time of impotency during their lifetime and often it is situational. Ninety percent of the cause lies in the man's head rather than in his physical condition. If impotency persists, additional information or help may be needed. (See *The Gift of Sex* by Joyce and Cliff Penner [Word] and *Intended for Pleasure* by Ed Wheat [Revell].)

Fear Is Our Foe

Causes of impotency include getting older and having less energy, anger and resentment toward women, fear of rejection, fear of being compared with other men, fear of not being able to satisfy his wife, fear of losing his erection or being unable to ejaculate, ridicule from his wife, guilt, unreasonable expectations, drugs, alcohol, poor physical condition and obesity, stress and too much on his mind! Take your pick! They all can bring on the same result.

Women have a multitude of questions about men's sexuality. One concerns men and masturbation. Are you aware that men worry about masturbation? All boys masturbate and it is to be hoped they understand that it is a normal part of the developmental process as they are growing up. But most men continue to masturbate throughout their lives, even happily married and sexually satisfied men. Some women are shocked at this fact and wonder what is wrong with the man who does it. Interestingly enough, some men who masturbate have the same questions. They may feel that it is all right for a child but for a grown man?

The reasons for men continuing to masturbate vary. Men may engage in masturbation because they are bored, they derive more satisfaction from their fantasies than from their wives, it is less of a hassle than the act itself, they are worried about work or so tired they could not sleep. It is a release for the man. Choosing to engage in the sexual fantasy, however, can have a negative effect upon the sexual relationship in the marriage. No real man or woman can ever measure up or compete with the Hollywood-style fantasy which our minds create. I suggest to both men and women that if they are going to engage in a sexual fantasy, they should fantasize about their own spouse and use that mental energy to develop more romance in their relationship. Become a creative lover with the person to whom you made your commitment when you married.

Men can learn that a quick sexual release every night cannot compare to a longer, romantic, sexual encounter twice a week. This will take working together to carve out the time, creating the atmosphere, having privacy and sufficient rest to enjoy the time. Reading the book *Solomon on Sex* by Joseph Dillow (Thomas Nelson) together can make a lot of this happen. The longer the foreplay and time taken in intercourse, the greater the intensity of the orgasm and the more intense pleasure for both men and women.

The Measure of a Man

Many women are concerned about the size of their bust lines. One woman remarked, "Men are better off than we are. They don't have to worry about the size of their sex apparatus." Wrong! Men do worry about the size of their penises! When an adolescent boy first encounters the locker room at school, he is embarrassed over the size of his penis. The myth goes something like this: You're more of a man if it's longer. Why? Longer is better and since men are competitive, why shouldn't the competition exist here with the size of one's "manhood"? When the average man's penis is flaccid, it may be anywhere from two and a half to four inches long. But when it is erect it is about six inches long. Sex researchers have discovered that, during an erection, a smaller penis extends more than a larger one, so the length evens out. But in the sexual act, which men need to realize, the size has absolutely nothing to do with the quality of sex and the partner's gratification. The circumference of the penis and the man's understanding of a woman's sexual response and what she needs is much more important.

Do men have a greater sex drive than women? No, they do not. Some have a high level of interest and enjoy sex every night whereas others are satisfied with sex twice a month. Dr. Barry Levine, a psychotherapist who lectures frequently in Los Angeles area colleges, states that the difference between men and women is not the sex drive, but socialization.

"Men are socialized to perform, to compete, to prove themselves with sex. Women are socialized to be sensual, to emphasize their feelings, to create a pleasing mood. When men are dissatisfied with a sexual relationship, they tend to seek out numerous partners in order to find the right one. A woman, on the other hand, is more likely to cope by abstaining. But while their behavior may differ, the basic sex drives of men and women essentially do not differ."[3]

Age and stress may also be factors in the levels of sexual desire.

Who Initiates?

Do men want a woman to take the lead sexually? The answer is *yes!* Verbal and nonverbal expressions help a man to feel needed and desired which creates a greater response toward his wife.

A recent study from the University of Connecticut conducted by Dr. Donald Mosher confirmed the fact that men usually have very positive reactions to women's sexual assertiveness. The old macho ideal of the male who always takes the lead was least appealing to men in this study. Men enjoyed taking turns and welcomed a woman's sexual initiative for the reasons cited and because it helped relieve them of the sole responsibility for sexual decisions and overtures.[4]

Not to be trite, but the key to understanding a man's sexual beliefs and responses is communication. You and your husband need to talk together about sex!

What can you do to encourage the man in your life to talk with you about sex? I feel it is important for not only husbands and wives to talk openly but for those who are dating and considering marriage. Open discussion about feelings, beliefs and attitudes concerning sex can be very beneficial. Could I make a suggestion? Ask your husband or special friend the following questions (after you've answered them yourself). You will have an enlightening discussion.

1. What are five adjectives you would use to describe your feelings about sex?

2. As a child, what was the first instruction you ever received about sex and who was it from?

3. How do you feel about talking with me at this moment about sex?

4. Is it more comfortable to talk with a woman about sex or a man? Why?

5. What do men fear the most about sex?

6. What do you think is the purpose of sex?

7. Do you have any questions concerning what I think or feel about sex?

8. Ask him to respond to the list of agree-disagree statements at the beginning of this chapter.

9. What do you think scripture teaches about sex?

10. What difference would being a Christian make in a couple's sexual relationship in marriage?

11. How often do you think about sex?

Now, read the following prayer to him and ask him how he feels about what was said and what he thinks about it. Conclude your discussion with the questions: "Have you ever thanked God for your sexuality? For the gift of being sexual?"

And by the way, have you? Sex is God's gift to all of us.

Thank you, O Creator, for the gift of sex to
enrich human life.
I rejoice in the wonder of a man and a maid,
     in the laughter of lovers,
     in the fragility of puppy love,
     in the excitement of "one-flesh."
Teach me to celebrate the beauty of bodies,
     the warmth of holding hands,
     the sweetness of Valentine's kisses,
     the joyfulness of sex.
Spare me from the anti-bodies
     Who are ashamed of themselves and your
     creation.
Waken me to the goodness of my body,
     And help me to cherish my body as your gift.
Melt the stiffness of my soul, and
Do not let me be ashamed of passion.
Help me to see that I can be
     sensual and pure,
     happy and holy,
     sexual and spiritual.
I affirm your creation, O God,
     the seeds spring forth,
     trees growing leaves,

Sex—What Else Do They Think About?   □   **201**

flowers blooming,
bodies filling out,
babies being born.
Remind me, O Creator, that sex comes from you
    And not from the devil
        No matter what the prudes may say.
Make me lighthearted, O God,
Let me be sensual but not sinful;
Let me dance and sing and be silly.
Keep my desires rich and real.
Do not let my nerves go dead
And my feelings get jaded.
Help me to celebrate sex as a good part of your creation.
Teach me to say: "Thank God for sex."[5]

Notes

Chapter 1

1. Joyce Brothers, *What Every Woman Should Know about Men* (New York: Ballantine Books, 1981), p. 5 adapted.
2. Georgia Witkin-Lanoil, *The Male Stress Syndrome* (New York: New Market Press, 1986), pp. 165, 167.
3. Peter and Evelyn Blitchington, *Understanding the Male Ego* (Nashville: Thomas Nelson Publishers, 1984), pp. 175–199 adapted.
4. Herb Goldberg, *The New Male* (New York: Signet Books, 1979), p. 17.
5. *Newsweek* (4 July 1976), pp. 30–31.
6. Goldberg, p. 14 adapted.
7. Ibid., p. 125.
8. Jerry Johnson, *What Every Woman Should Know about a Man* (Grand Rapids: Zondervan, 1981), pp. 104–105.

Chapter 2

1. Joyce Brothers, *What Every Woman Should Know about Men* (New York: Ballantine Books, 1981), pp. 31–34 adapted. Jacquelyn Wonder and Priscilla Donovan, *Whole Brain Thinking* (New York: William Morrow and Company, 1984), pp. 18–34 adapted.
2. Ibid., pp. 48–50 adapted.
3. Kevin Leman, *The Birth Order Book* (Old Tappan, NJ: Fleming H. Revell, 1984), pp. 11–38 adapted.
4. G. Karl Knoig, *Brothers and Sisters* (Blowelt, NY: St. George Books, 1963), p. 63 adapted.
5. Barbara A. Sullivan, *First Born, Second Born* (Chosen Books, Old Tappan NJ: Fleming H. Revell, 1983), pp. 76–77 adapted.
6. Leman, pp. 72–76 adapted.
7. Bradford Wilson and George Edington, *First Child, Second Child* (New York: McGraw-Hill Book Company, 1983).
8. Pam Hait, "Birth Order and Relationships," *Sunday Woman* (12 September 1982), p. 4.
9. Rudolf Dreikurs, *The Challenge of Parenthood* (New York: Hawthorne Books, Inc., 1985), p. 47.
10. Leman, p. 10 adapted.

Chapter 3
1. William S. Appleton, M.D., *Fathers and Daughters* (New York: Doubleday & Co., Inc., 1981), p. 41.
2. Ibid., p. 21.
3. Ibid., pp. 1–30 adapted.
4. Hugh Missildine, *Your Inner Child of the Past* (New York: Simon and Schuster, 1968), p. 59.
5. (Material in this section was adapted from H. Norman Wright, *Making Peace with Your Past* (Old Tappan, NJ: Fleming H. Revell, 1985). For additional assistance, see Chapter 6 from *Making Peace with Your Past* by the author and *Finding Inner Security* by Jan Congo (Regal Books).
6. Howard Halpern, *Cutting Loose—An Adult Guide to Coming to Terms with Your Parents* (New York: Simon and Schuster, 1977), p. 1.

Chapter 4
1. F.F. Furstenberg, J.L. Peterson, C. Nord and N. Zill, "Life Course of Children of Divorce: Marital Disruption in Parental Contact," *American Sociological Review* (1983: 656–668), p. 48.
2. S. Hite, *The Hite Report on Male Sexuality* (New York: Knopf, 1981), p. 17 adapted.
3. J. Arcana, *Every Mother's Son—The Role of Mothers in the Making of Men* (Garden City, NY: Doubleday & Co., 1983), p. 143 adapted.
4. J. Sternbach, "The Masculinization Process," unpublished paper, RFD Box 607, Vineyard Haven, MA 02568.
5. Samuel Osherson, *Finding Our Fathers* (New York: The Free Press, 1986), pp. 31–36 adapted.
6. Ken Druck, *The Secrets Men Keep* (New York: Doubleday & Co., 1985), pp. 54–61 adapted.

Chapter 5
1. Michael McGill, *The McGill Report on Intimacy* (San Francisco: Harper & Row, 1985), pp. 173–174.
2. Joel D. Block, *Friendship* (New York: Collier Books, 1980), pp. 53–55 adapted.
3. Ibid., p. 55 adapted.
4. Ibid., p. 56 adapted.
5. Ken Druck, *The Secrets Men Keep* (New York: Doubleday & Co., 1985), pp. 101–102 adapted.
6. Ibid., pp. 112–114.
7. McGill, pp. 176–177 adapted.
8. Druck, pp. 103–106 adapted.

Chapter 6
1. Herb Goldberg, *The Hazards of Being Male* (New York: New American Library, 1976), pp. 44–45.
2. Ibid., pp. 57–58 adapted.
3. Ken Olson, *Hey Man! Open Up and Live* (New York: Fawcett, 1978), pp. 147–48.

4. Ken Druck, *The Secrets Men Keep* (New York: Doubleday & Co., 1985), pp. 39–40 adapted.
5. Michael McGill, *The McGill Report on Male Intimacy* (San Francisco: Harper & Row, 1985), pp. 43–77 adapted.
6. Ibid., p. 74.
7. Ibid., pp. 205–206.
8. Jerry Schmidt and Raymond Block, *The Emotional Side of Men* (Eugene, OR: Harvest House, 1983), pp. 84–85.

Chapter 7
1. Robert and Dorothy Grover Bolton, *Social Style/Management Style* (New York: Amacom, 1984), pp. 20–24, 33 adapted.

Chapter 8
1. Gerard Egan, *You and Me* (Monterey, CA: Brooks Cole, 1977), p. 85.

Chapter 9
1. Dante, *Inferno*, Canto One.
2. Georgia Witkin-Lanoil, *The Male Stress Syndrome* (New York: New Market Press, 1986), p. 186 adapted.
3. Richard Olson, *Midlife; A Time to Discover, A Time to Decide* (Valley Forge, PA: Judson Press, 1980), p. 62, as quoted in Laurence Peters, *Peter's Quotations* (New York: William Morrow and Company, Inc., 1977), p. 330.
4. Sally Conway, *You and Your Husband's Midlife Crisis* (Elgin, IL: David C. Cook, 1980), p. 200.
5. Book iv, line 73, John Milton, *Paradise Lost.*
6. Samuel Osherson, *Finding Our Fathers* (New York: The Free Press, 1986), pp. 72–95 adapted.
7. Michael McGill, *The 40 to 60-Year-Old Male* (New York: Simon and Schuster, 1980), pp. 42–52 adapted.
8. Osherson, p. 96.
9. McGill, pp. 248–265 adapted.
10. Stephen A. Shapiro, *Manhood—A New Definition* (New York: G.P. Putnam & Sons, 1984), p. 183.

Chapter 10
1. 1984 Statistical Abstracts of the United States.
2. Archibald Hart, *Adrenalin and Stress* (Waco, TX: Word, 1986), p. 30.
3. Georgia Witkin-Lanoil, *The Male Stress Syndrome* (New York: New Market Press, 1986), pp. 5–6 adapted.
4. Ibid., pp. 12–20 adapted.
5. Ibid., p. 129.
6. Ibid., pp. 25–26 and Archibald Hart.
7. Georgia Witkin-Lanoil, p. 33.
8. H. Norman Wright, *How to Have a Creative Crisis* (Waco, TX: Word, 1986).
9. Georgia Witkin-Lanoil, pp. 71–73 adapted.
10. Ibid., pp. 77–78 adapted and Keith Sehnert, *Stress Unstress* (Minneapolis: Augsburg Publishing House, 1981), pp. 74–75 adapted.

Chapter 11
1. Dr. Ken Druck, *The Secrets Men Keep* (New York: Doubleday & Co., 1985), p. 132.
2. Ibid., pp. 135–136 adapted.

Chapter 12
1. Dan Kiley, *The Wendy Dilemma* (New York: Avon Books, 1985), pp. 47–48 adapted.
2. —————, *The Peter Pan Syndrome* (New York: Avon Books, 1983), pp. 9–11 adapted.
3. Ibid., pp. 234–240 adapted.
4. Susan Forward and Joan Torres, *Men Who Hate Women and the Women Who Love Them* (New York: Bantam Books, 1986), p. 163. Adapted.
5. Ibid., pp. 168–169. Adapted.
6. Ibid., pp. 169–170. Adapted.

Chapter 13
1. Michael McGill, *The McGill Report on Male Intimacy* (New York: Harper & Row, 1985), pp. 188–189 adapted.
2. Ibid., p. 58 adapted.
3. Kathleen McCoy, "What Every Man Wishes His Wife Knew" (*Redbook* Magazine, October, 1985), pp. 142–3, 210.
4. Ibid.
5. Henry Hollis, Jr., *Thank God for Sex* (Nashville: Broadman Press, 1975), pp. 55–56.

Study Guide

How to Use This Book

The questions and exercises in this study guide are designed for individual study which will in turn lead to group interaction. Thus, they may be used either as a guide for individual meditation or group discussion. During your first group meeting we suggest that you set aside a few minutes at the outset in which individual group members introduce themselves.

You may want to begin each meeting with a different question designed to cause participants to think and share information not previously considered. Use just one question, but go around your group and ask each person to share. Here are some suggested questions:

1. What is your favorite smell?
2. What is your favorite sight?
3. What is your favorite touch?
4. What is your favorite taste?
5. What is your favorite sound?
6. What do your favorite senses say about you?
7. What is the first gift that you can remember receiving?
8. What are two adjectives you would use to describe yourself?
9. What two adjectives would the man in your life use to describe you?
10. In the past six months, what passage of scripture has meant the most to you and why?
11. If you could reach out and heal someone one day, who would it be?

If possible, it is a good idea to rotate leadership responsibility among the group members. However, if one individual is particularly gifted as a discussion leader, elect or appoint that person to guide the discussions each week. Remember, the leader's responsibility is simply to guide the discussion and stimulate interaction. He or she should never dominate the proceedings. Rather, the leader should encourage all members of the group to participate, expressing their individual views. He or she should seek to keep the discussion on track, but encourage lively discussion.

If one of the purposes of your group meeting is to create a caring community, it is a good idea to set aside some time for sharing individual concerns and prayers for one another. This can take the form of both silent and spoken petitions and praise.

Chapter 1. What Is a Man?

1. Make a list of ten stereotypes that women have of men. How do these stereotypes affect your responses to men?
2. List what you feel are three or four of the main concerns of the man in your life.
3. If you were to ask a man how he would describe what a man is, what do you think he would say? Why not ask one this next week?
4. Share your responses to the ten questions listed at the end of Chapter 1 and be sure to give an illustration or example with your "yes" or "no" answers.

Chapter 2. Why Is He That Way?

1. In this chapter, the following statement is made: "We are born male and female and raised and trained to be masculine or feminine." What do you think and why?
2. How do you feel that left brain/right brain differences are apparent in your relationships with men?
3. List your brothers and sisters in their birth order or your own children in their order. How do their characteristics match the characteristics mentioned in this chapter?
4. Describe the qualities or characteristics of the most significant man in your life. Why do you feel he is that way? How do his characteristics affect his spiritual life and relationship with Jesus Christ?

Chapter 3. The First Man in Your Life

1. What were (or are) ten adjectives you would use to describe your father?
2. Describe a time in which you felt close to your father.
3. Describe a time in which you felt distant from your father.
4. If you could say anything you've ever wanted to say to your father, what would it be?

5. Describe how your relationship with your father has affected your relationship with men today.
6. Do any of the following words describe your situation as you were raised? Overcoercion, oversubmission, overindulgence, perfectionistic, rejected?
7. Share your responses to the questions listed at the end of this chapter.

Chapter 4. The Other Man in Your Man's Life

1. How would the significant men in your life personally answer the twelve questions in the first part of this chapter?
2. Which of the father types mentioned in the chapter best described the following:
    1. Your own father?
    2. Your significant man's father?
    3. If you are married, your own husband?
(The admiral, the nice father, the professor father, the angry martyr father, the hard-working father, the macho father, and the loving father.)
3. At the end of the description of each of these fathers there is "a question for you, the reader." Share your response to these questions.
4. During this week (if you have not already done so) ask the man in your life the questions at the end of the chapter. But share right now what you feel his responses will be.

Chapter 5. Men and Their Friends

1. Share your response to the questions at the beginning of this chapter with one another. (Note: this *could* take a significant amount of time.)
2. Describe the walls you see men erecting in their lives. What can you do to penetrate these walls?
3. Several types of friends are described in this chapter. Classify the friends of the man in your life, using these categories.
4. How would you describe the type of friend you are to the man in your life? How would he describe the type of friend you are?
5. Describe how the man in your life would respond if he had lost a close friend as the man in the story at the beginning of the chapter did.

Chapter 6. Feeling the Great Male Struggle

1. Describe the various feelings the man in your life shares with you and how these are shared.
2. What are some of the masks you have seen men use to hide their feelings?
3. Which emotions do you wish the man in your life would share and how can you help him to do so?
4. Describe the feelings you share with men to which it is difficult for them to respond.

5. Describe a time in which you heard a "typical non-feeling man" share his feelings. What caused this to occur?

Chapter 7. How to Communicate with a Man

1. Circle the following words which best describe you and underline the words that best describe the man in your life:
Condenser, amplifier, straight-line communicator, around-the-barn communicator, visual, auditory, kinesthetic, analytical, amiable, expressive, driver. How do these differences affect your communication with your man?
2. Do you feel more comfortable with someone who communicates in the same way or differently than you? Why do you feel this way?
3. Describe how you will begin to speak the language of another person this week.
4. Select two of the scriptures listed at the end of the chapter and write out specifically how you will put these into practice this next week in your communication.

Chapter 8. Helping Men Share Their Feelings

1. Describe how the man in your life would like you to change your pattern and style of communication. Describe how you would like him to change.
2. Describe how you answered the eleven questions in the beginning portion of this chapter.
3. Share your own response to the sentence completion questions that follow.
4. How do you feel about the suggestions under the heading, "Within a Request—do the Following"?
5. Describe the plan you are going to follow to help the man in your life share more of his feelings with you.

Chapter 9. High Noon in a Man's Life

1. Describe how you feel about your age at this time in your life.
2. Who are the men you know who are in midlife and how are they responding to this stage? Describe how your own father handled this stage.
3. If the man in your life is in midlife or has not reached it, which of the following causes of a crisis are affecting him or may affect him?
Goal Gap, the Dream, Search for Adventure, Step Aside, The Empty Nest, Vanity and Virility, or Meeting Mortality.
4. Are you employed outside the home? How does your husband or the man in your life respond to this? If you are not employed and decided to work, how would the man respond?
5. What concerns you the most about men in midlife?
6. On a scale of 0–10, rate your own level of dependency on the man in your life:

very independent   *average*   *dependent*

What do you build your identity upon?
(I would encourage you to read *Finding Inner Security* by Jan Congo [Regal]).

Chapter 10. Men under Stress—It Affects You, Too!

1. Describe the most recent stressful experience for your man and how he responded to it. What would you have suggested that he do?
2. What are the five main stressors in your life at the present time?
3. What are the five main stressors in your man's life at the present time?
4. What is your opinion concerning the idea that being out of control is one of the biggest sources of stress for men?
5. What are four suggestions you would make to someone else to help them handle stress in their lives?
6. What are four passages from the Word of God you would suggest to put into practice in order to handle the stresses of life?
7. List four helpful responses the man in your life would like from you when he is stressed out.

Chapter 11. The Arena

1. Give your initial response to the following sentence completion questions. Then share these with the others in your group.
    1. The way I feel about my man's work is . . . .
    2. His work affects him by . . . .
    3. He believes his work is . . . .
    4. I believe his work is . . . .
2. In what way do you see men "defined by their work"?
3. Have you asked the man in your life what he likes the most about his work and what he dislikes? What he gains from his involvement in work and what he loses by his involvement? Describe how you feel he would answer.
4. Have you ever felt you were competing with a man's work? How did you feel and what did you do?
5. What can you do to encourage a man to gain his identity from sources other than his work?

Chapter 12. Men Who Never Grow Up

1. Describe the men you've known who fit the Peter Pan syndrome. How did you feel about that man's responses and the way you responded?
2. How do you feel about the suggestions given to respond to such a man? What else would you suggest?

3. What is the likelihood that a man like this will change? What could you do if you see your son manifest these characteristics?

4. There are many concepts listed from the book, *Men Who Hate Women*. What was your reaction to both the theme of the book and the concepts? What options does a woman have who is married to this type of man or works for one? (Perhaps someone from your group could read the book and present a comprehensive review.)

Chapter 13. Sex—What Else Do They Think About?

1. Respond to the fourteen questions at the beginning of this chapter. Share whether you agree or disagree and *why*.

2. Share your answers to the eleven questions concerning sex in the section under "Who Initiates?"
(This may take more than one group session)

3. Close your meeting by having one person read the prayer, "Thanking God for Sex."

H. NORMAN WRIGHT is a widely known
marriage counselor, trainer of counselors, and
longtime professor of counseling at Biola
University and Talbot Seminary. He is founder and
director of Christian Marriage Enrichment and
Family Counseling and Enrichment in Santa Ana,
California. His more than fifty books include
Communication: Key to Your Marriage, Crisis Counseling,
and *How to Have a Creative Crisis.* He is also the
author of *Self-Talk, Imagery and Prayer* in the
Resources for Christian Counseling series.